HOW TO SOLVE YOUR DECORATING PROBLEMS

Barbara Taylor Bradford

SIMON AND SCHUSTER · NEW YORK

Designed by Eve Metz

Manufactured in the United States of America

1   2   3   4   5   6   7   8   9   10

Library of Congress Cataloging in Publication Data

Bradford, Barbara Taylor.
    How to solve your decorating problems.

    Includes index.
    1.   Interior decoration—Handbooks, manuals, etc.
I.   Title.
NK2110.B68   747′.8′8   75-37548
ISBN 0-671-22202-3

FOR MEL AND JOAN BLUTTER WITH MY LOVE

CONTENTS

INTRODUCTION

Almost every home has some kind of decorating problem and whether that problem is large or small, it can appear difficult to the non-professional.

Yet there are basic solutions for almost every decorating problem, solutions that are relatively simple for anyone who knows and understands a few of the basic decorating rules. Some of the solutions given here are even budget-minded, and this is certainly an important consideration these days.

The most common decorating problems, and the ones you are most likely to come across yourself, are dealt with in this book. Hundreds of letters from readers of my nationally syndicated column have pin-pointed these problems and made me increasingly aware that they are very basic and prevalent in almost every type of home.

The aim of this book is to focus on these very common problems and give you a variety of workable solutions for them, solutions which are fairly simple to do, practical, effective, and economical as well. In each of the chapters I deal with specific difficulties and show you ways to overcome them successfully.

For example, whether you live in an apartment or a house, you may have to deal with an oddly proportioned window, an awkwardly shaped room, lack of space, old-fashioned kitchens and bathrooms. Or you may be seeking some way to give a dull room focus or to revitalize a tired room suffering from the blahs. Perhaps you have to plan a room to accommodate two or more children; or you may have a problem arranging the furniture or creating an effective color scheme.

Whatever your problems, there are solutions for every one of them—formulas which help you to handle a specific problem individually, thus avoiding the expense of redecorating a room completely. Naturally this is of vital importance today, when few people can afford to create a whole new scheme simply to overcome one inherent difficulty overlooked at the outset of decorating, or to spend the money correcting a bad decorating mistake. It is also much easier and less tiring to decorate step by step, treating each problem individually as you have the time . . . and the money.

This book shows you how to do this successfully, pinpointing typical problems in many "before" photographs of rooms and demonstrating in photographs of the redecorated rooms how the problem has been effectively treated.

It is a book full of good ideas created by leading interior designers, many of them oriented toward small budgets. It will help you to solve your decorating problems intelligently and with self-confidence.

1 · Decorating Difficult Windows

A great number of windows common to apartments and houses are difficult to decorate, either because of their peculiar shape and size or because of awkward placement on a given wall.

These difficult windows include bows, bays, skylights, cathedral windows, French door windows, walls of windows and others that are too close together, oddly positioned, too small or too large for the actual dimensions of the room. They are difficult because they do not meet the given or accepted standards of the average window, but of course they can be decorated attractively once you understand the interior architectural problems they pose.

Like any other decorating problem, the difficult window can easily be brought into line by following a few basic design rules. These rules help to simplify your task, because they show you how to decorate the difficult window in the easiest and most effective way. And once you know and understand these rules you will have that much more confidence to go ahead. You will also avoid making mistakes that can be time consuming and costly to correct.

Basically windows have several functions in a room. Their purpose is to let in natural light and ventilation and to permit a view to be seen, if one exists. However, they are also a decorative element in a room and thus have to be treated effectively, so that they underscore or complement the overall decor. Many people think it is sufficient to give a window curtains and leave it at that, but this is simply not the case. Curtains may be inappropriate for the style and shape of the window, its size and the way it operates; they may be wrong for the functions of the window within the room, as well as unsuitable for the overall style of the room. This is why it is vital to consider all the alternative treatments available.

Before you select a treatment, it is a good idea to analyze both the room and the window. First you should view the window and the room together as one entity. Any kind of window, whether it is difficult or not, is an essential part of the background and should be decorated as

11

such. It has to blend with the treatment you have used for the walls, and the decorative style of the furnishings. Look at the colors and materials you have put on the walls and then consider all the colors and materials available for window treatments. In this way you will be able to decide which colors and textures can be coordinated most successfully with the walls for the best results.

Once you have examined the room and the window as one whole entity, analyze the window by itself. Make a checklist of all the different types of treatments you can use and select the one that works the best for the size, shape and function of the window. At this time you must also decide whether you want the window to blend inconspicuously into the background composed of walls and floor, whether you wish it to add a degree of design interest or even stand out dramatically as a strong focal point. When you have decided on the most suitable type of treatment, its style, color and material, you can set about decorating your difficult window.

Before you begin decorating, however, consider the amount of money the window treatment will cost in relation to how much you can afford to spend. It may well be that the particular treatment you prefer is going to be out of line with your financial means. For example, let's say you want to decorate a series of windows along one wall of a bedroom and have decided that floor-to-ceiling draperies covering the entire wall will be the most effective treatment. Unless you are a clever home sewer and can make the draperies yourself, you will find this is quite an expensive job to tackle. You not only have the price of yards and yards of fabric, plus the lining fabric necessary, but also the cost of making and install- ing the draperies, as well as the price of the hardware required. The total sum involved might be too prohibitive for your budget.

In this instance you have several alternatives. You can select another less costly treatment or you can adapt the draperies so that they cost less. To save money you must cut corners. You can buy a cheaper fabric and dispense with the lining material altogether. However, if you do this you will have to add plain window shades to provide privacy and room-darkening qualities. Even so, inexpensive window shades are readily available and this combination is an economical solution. You will save on the fabrics involved and also on the actual making, since unlined draperies are not so costly as those that are lined.

Another alternative is to use sets of floor-to-ceiling draperies, tied back or falling loose, that simply frame each window and remain station- ary at all times. These draperies are actually clever fakes that give the effect of real draperies, but which do not close to cover the entire set of windows and the wall space in between. Obviously this kind of treatment requires even less fabric and again the need for lining is eliminated. Room-darkening window shades would have to be added for the obvious reasons, but once again the overall saving is enormous. In other words, there are always alternative solutions for every window, however difficult it is, and you should never be dismayed if your first choice proves to be too expensive. There are a wealth of products available today to make your decorating task much easier and interior designers are always coming up with ingenious ideas that solve difficult window problems. Many of these solutions are shown in the picture stories further along in this chapter, and they should help you to decorate that difficult window effectively.

BASIC RULES FOR DECORATING WINDOWS

When you are analyzing the room and the difficult window, it's a good idea to bear in mind a few rules that will make your decorating all that much easier. Copy the list of rules given here in a small notebook so that you have it handy at all times. You can also use the notebook for making other notations of ideas for your difficult window.

1. The treatment should be as functional as possible, permitting air and light to circulate. If necessary it should filter glare; it should also provide room-darkening qualities and privacy when these are required, such as in a bedroom.

2. The treatment you select must be in keeping with your budget.

3. The scale of the treatment must be balanced to the actual size of the window as well as the overall dimensions of the room.

4. The treatment must be practical for the way the window opens and closes.

5. The type of treatment you select must not interfere with air conditioner or radiator if these are part of the window area.

6. The treatment should be practical for the purpose of the room and its function.

7. The decorative effect must be coordinated to the period of furniture used and the overall decorative style of the room.

8. The style of the treatment must blend with the interior architecture of the room.

HOW TO SOLVE YOUR DECORATING PROBLEMS

PROBLEM: Two old-fashioned, double-hung windows, exposed radiator and awkwardly placed protruding beams.

SOLUTION: Floor-to-ceiling sheer curtains balanced by floor-to-ceiling draperies, the combination covering entire wall.

The double-hung sash windows adjacent to each other in this apartment living room are typical of the kind usually found in old buildings. Apart from their unattractive appearance they look out onto a dismal view. Other problems on this window wall are the exposed, ugly radiator and the two protruding side beams.

Interior designer Virginia Frankel solved the problem of this difficult window by treating the entire wall. In this way she not only camouflaged the unattractive window and the view, but the radiator and protruding beams as well. She began by hanging floor-to-ceiling sheer white curtains in front of the adjacent windows. These sheers were then balanced by floor-length draperies hung at each end and in the center. The green-and-white modern fabric adds pattern and color interest, while hiding central window strut and wall beams. Apart from their camouflaging qualities, the curtain-drapery combination helps to give the room a feeling of extra height and depth. The designer selected this treatment for several other reasons. It introduces an uncluttered modern feeling, which was essential for the mixture of modern furniture and the sleek vinyl floor; it adds softness and makes a good backdrop for the yellow striped sofa. For additional movement at this end of the room, Virginia Frankel used a tall etagere and a floor lamp.

PROBLEM: *Large-scale, curving bay split up by five leaded-glass transoms, five individual windows set in heavy frames and built-in unit below.*

SOLUTION: *Tailored window shades, plants and panel track lights.*

This bay window in a town house presented problems because of its grand scale, its curving shape and the five separate windows set within the area, which cut up the overall sweep of the bay. Adding to this divided feeling were leaded-glass transoms above and the built-in unit below containing radiators and air conditioner. All of these elements had to be carefully considered in the initial planning stages, so that they could be handled in the most effective way. Interior designer Susan Hubbell dismissed the idea of using floor-length draperies because of the protruding unit; she also bypassed sets of short curtains because they would have created a fussy look and emphasized the separateness of the individual windows. Instead the designer decided to play up the structural look of the windows and also make a feature of the leaded transoms. She began by removing white paint from the wood frames and built-in unit and then restored the handsome wood patina of the bay. The actual window treatment is composed of individual window shades set within the frames. These are in a bright blue bordered with braid in primary colors and finished with wood ring pulls painted bright yellow. The plain shades fit neatly and are highly practical, finishing just above the built-in unit. They do not compete with the handsome wood surround or the leaded transoms, and in fact allow these elements to stand out as attractive features of the bay. To soften the tailored feeling created by the window shades Susan Hubbell hung plants from the ceiling at different levels in front of the three center windows. The ceiling light track was the final addition and it not only provides necessary illumination in the window area but also spotlights the bay's natural drama. A difficult window so becomes a handsome backdrop for the modern furniture arrangement and also an interesting focal point in the room.

PROBLEM: *Old-fashioned, unattractive bow with three differently sized windows, too large for dimension of the wall.*

SOLUTION: *White paint, white window shades and clean-lined furniture.*

An old-fashioned bow window can often be turned into an eye-catching element in a room. Witness this charming relaxation corner in a bedroom, which started out as a rather unattractive window area that broke up the flow of the main wall in a small bedroom of a Victorian house. Interior designer Carl Fuchs painted the entire window area white and for contrast used a plum-colored paint in the rest of the room. This pristine crispness was abetted by the white room-darkening shades, which the designer stenciled in a stylized shell and ribbon design in hot pink and plum. By painting the bow white and using white shades the wall and windows are seemingly pushed out, so that the area seems larger than it really is, by visual illusion. It became the ideal spot for the chaise, a Victorian relic painted white and treated to a mattress and cushion upholstered in white and pink fabric. An old night stand was also white-painted and makes a practical telephone stand. For extra decorative effect on the shades, real scallop shells were used as shade pulls. The stenciled design of the shades was repeated as a border on the white floor and the whole was then heavily shellacked for wearability. Both the window treatment and the floor are inexpensive budget ideas which are relatively easy to do yourself. All the furniture in the bedroom are junk shop finds refinished to fit in with the overall decorative theme.

PROBLEM: Two-level window wall composed of half windows above a radiator and floor-to-ceiling sliding glass door opening onto terrace.

SOLUTION: Vertical blinds cut to fit both levels and which open back to allow access to door.

This two-level window wall, a typical design found in many apartments, was suavely handled with a sleek treatment composed of two sets of short and long vertical blinds by designer Peg Walker. Translucent and made of white shade cloth, they take the two-level window wall in stride so nimbly that they cover the half window and give easy access to the sliding glass door to the terrace at the same time. They also permit a complete play of light and view, according to the way they are rotated or pulled back altogether to one side. Because of their sleek simplicity they blend well with the modern architecture and furnishings, as well as solving the difficult decorating problem so easily. Plants help to disguise the protruding air conditioner as does the furniture arrangement of chairs and tables lined up at the window end of the room.

PROBLEM: A wall of small metal-trimmed modern windows in a room with a traditional decorative character.

SOLUTION: Roman shades, wooden beams, a long window seat and plants.

A wall of small, metal-trimmed modern windows was the stumbling block in this living room. Apart from being unimportant and unattractive, the modern windows were out of character with the overall traditional mood being developed for the room. Fortunately interior designer Raymond Pastor was decorating this room from scratch and so was able to plan the windows at the outset. He was also saved the cost and trouble of correcting previous mistakes. However, his ideas can be adapted for a room already decorated providing they suit the character of the room in question. The designer decided to alter the character and style of the windows totally by traditionalizing them to blend with the mood he wanted to create throughout. At the same time he turned the wall into a charming, highly original and eye-catching focus of interest. He at once introduced a period look by running three wooden beams down from the protruding ceiling beam to the window sill, to match the beams he had put up on the other walls. He then took a green, yellow and blue fabric coordinated to the wall covering and had this made into three Roman shades. These help to block out the unattractive metal trimming on the windows. Once the windows had been treated he built a long, wide and low window seat along the entire length of the wall. This he decorated in the most imaginative way. He created a lush-looking indoor garden composed of all manner of plants in interesting planters, dried flowers, grasses, reeds and feathers in a basket and a large barrel. These were backed up by a collection of stones grouped to simulate the feeling of a rock garden. He interspersed several large colorful cushions amongst the plants to provide comfortable seating in the window area. To further the country mood, a variety of hanging plants were suspended from the ceiling and the window beams; others were arranged on the window sill. Apart from its decorative impact, the window wall dispenses with the need for additional furniture in this part of the living room. The window seat is practical since it provides additional seating space when required; plants are simply removed when more space is required.

9. The treatment must be easy to keep clean and maintain.

10. The treatment must be appropriate for the kind of natural light coming into the room, such as cold northern and eastern light, warm southern and western light.

11. The color of the treatment should harmonize with the color scheme of the room.

12. The texture of the treatment should blend with the other textures in the room, whether this is fabric, wood or any other material.

By paying attention to the above basics you will be able to make an accurate assessment about the window as you go along and you will also be totally aware of the ingredients required to create a successful treatment. Decorating a difficult window correctly is really only a problem when you are unsure of what you are doing. Once you know the design rules, you will have self-confidence in yourself as a decorator— because you *know* you have the expertise to prevent your making mistakes.

TYPES OF DIFFICULT WINDOWS

Difficult windows are usually those which do not fit into the two standard categories generally found in homes today. These two standards are the double-hung window with upper and lower sashes that open up or down, and the horizontally sliding window with two sashes side by side that slide across to open. Almost any other style fits into the "difficult" category. However, I think it's worth mentioning here that both double-hung and horizontally sliding windows can also often be difficult to decorate. Such windows can be problematical if there are more than one on a wall; if they are peculiarly placed, either too high or too low; or if they are too close together.

For instance, sometimes you will find a double-hung window next to a French door and this creates an unbalanced short-high look; often two horizontally sliding windows may flank a fixed pane of glass producing an overly large expanse of glass to be decorated. But as I pointed out earlier, there is always a solution which will bring the window into decorative line with the overall style of the room. Before looking at some of these solutions, let's consider those difficult windows which are the most common and which you are most likely to find in today's homes.

BAY OR BOW   This is usually composed of one large window or three or more windows that project out from the walls of the house. When there are two, three or more windows these are set at an angle and so form a bay. A bow window is always semi-circular in shape. Normally double-hung windows are used in a bow or bay shape. It is not so much the windows themselves which are difficult to decorate, but rather the overall shape of the entire window area. This is particularly so when there is a protruding window seat, ledge or air-conditioner–radiator unit.

SKYLIGHT   This can be a large or small window set into the roof or on a sloping wall that forms an eave. Sometimes they are of fixed panes of glass that do not open; others are of panes of glass that open outwards.

CATHEDRAL   This is usually a slanted window set high in a wall very close to a cathedral-shaped ceiling. This type of window is quite common in A-frame houses.

FRENCH   These are actually door windows which open like doors and are usually the same standard size as doors. They are made of one or more panes of glass.

PICTURE   This is one very large window made of one or more fixed panes of glass. Sometimes it has movable sections.

RANCH   These are wide windows (or window) set high on the wall. Very often their proportion is poor in relation to the size of the wall. They either slide open or open in and out. Sometimes the ranch style window is referred to as the hopper.

DORMER   This is a small window, usually vertically shaped, set high in a wall and projecting out from the house in an alcove-like extension. They are normally double-hung windows.

CLERESTORY   These are small, shallow windows set near the ceiling; they normally follow the roof line.

CORNER   This is most often composed of two windows that come close together on two adjoining walls that form the corner of a room. They can be of any style.

WALL OF GLASS   This is usually composed of fixed and movable panels. The movable sections can include sliding glass doors or one-panel awning windows. Often the fixed panels are of unusual shape, such as a floor-to-ceiling slanting panel rising to a cathedral ceiling.

TOO SMALL/TOO LARGE   These windows can be of any style, but they are out of proportion to the dimension of the wall and the room as a whole, creating an unbalanced look.

AWKWARDLY POSITIONED   This type of window is badly placed in the room. It can be too high or too low on the wall, set too close to a corner, a door or a fireplace, even a staircase.

ADJOINING   These windows are generally set too close to each other and break up the flowing look of the wall. Adjoining windows can be two or as many as five or six.

VIEWLESS   This window is difficult inasmuch as it faces onto a poor view or none at all, such as a brick wall or another building.

WRONG STYLE   This kind of window may be the correct style for the architecture of the room, but wrong for the decorative look to be created in the room. For example, a modern window style is out of character in a room furnished with period furniture; an old-fashioned window looks out of place when a traditional room is transformed with modern pieces.

APPROPRIATE TREATMENTS

Let us now consider appropriate treatments for these difficult windows, ones which solve the inherent decorating problem effectively, easily and on a reasonable budget.

BAY OR BOW   The main problem here is the circular or angled shape of the window area. However, there are several simple treatments which are ideal solutions for overcoming this difficulty. If the wall space below the window is not broken up by a protruding window seat, window ledge or heating-cooling unit, you can create a soft yet handsome effect with floor-length draperies in almost any style, providing your selected style is suitable for the overall decorative mood of the room. If the room is furnished with modern, then stay with simple, tailored draperies with a French heading; if the room has traditional overtones go with a slightly dressier period style and add a valance or jabot as a heading. The floor-length draperies can be tied back or left falling straight and loose, depending on your taste, and they can be combined with sheers or window shades if you wish. Curving ceiling track now available makes it easy to hang draperies so that they follow the circular flow of the bow; other specially shaped track, or straight track mounted at angles, enables you to hang draperies so that they fit the shape of a bay. And after all, it is the shape of these windows that gives them their basic charm.

When you have a bay or bow with a protruding window seat, ledge or heating-cooling unit below, it is usually advisable to utilize a treatment that does not interfere with any of these elements. Whichever treatment you select, it must stop short at the sill level. If draperies are your preference, you can use several styles: tie-backs, Priscillas (criss-crossed at the top and tied back) or straight, loose curtains.

Window shades, either alone or in combination with draperies, are also effective, since they can be made to fit the shape of the windows. They introduce a clean, sleek look and of course they do not interfere with any elements that might protrude from the wall below. The window shades available today are highly decorative and work well on their own. Colors are unlimited and there is a wide choice of textures which produce interesting effects. There are also specially treated window shades which are easy to laminate yourself. Through a simple iron-on process you can attach fabric to these shades; in this instance, it is wise to select a fabric used elsewhere in the room, either for upholstery or draperies, or one coordinated to a wallpaper. Any ordinary plain window shade can be decorated with painted or stenciled patterns, decals or cut-outs of wallpaper and fabric, while colorful braid will add a good-looking finishing trim. Unusual shade pulls, such as old-fashioned metal drawer pulls, shells, silk, wool or rope tassels and brass or wood curtain rings all help to enhance the simple window shade. Incidentally, these can be used with or without a valance, depending on your taste and the style of the room. When selecting the color of your window shade be sure that it blends into the overall color scheme of the room, and especially with drapery and window seat fabrics if these are used. Naturally, the same rule applies if you are using short draperies. The color should harmonize with the total scheme, upholstery on the window seat and in the rest of the room.

SKYLIGHT   The main problem with this kind of window is that it is set into a roof, ceiling or sloping eave. This immediately prohibits the use of almost every type of treatment, except those that fit flush to the skylight itself. The best treatments to use are window shades, Austrian blinds or shirred curtains. All of these are flat and can be easily attached to the window's frame; each one of them can be opened to let in light when necessary; all of them permit the skylight itself to be opened and closed. If the room with a skylight is dark or if you want lots of natural light to filter in continuously, select a sheer fabric for the shirred curtain or Austrian blind, a translucent texture for the window shade. When daylight is not a consideration, you can choose heavier fabrics.

An alternative to the three treatments just mentioned is a structural treatment that remains permanently in position. However, you can only utilize this when you are not concerned with the circulation of air or lots of natural light, as this type of treatment hides the window completely. One of the most effective I have seen recently was created by an interior designer who transformed an attic into a charming library in period style. The designer first attached narrow strip lighting at the top and bottom of the skylight casing and then covered the whole with a leaded, stained-glass window, which she picked up cheaply in a junk shop. The stained-glass window was screwed into position on the sloping ceiling and then finished with strips of molding painted to match the ceiling. During the day natural light filters through softly, while at night, when the strip lighting is on, the skylight becomes a jewel-toned focal point. Panels of translucent plastic, available in a variety of colors, can be used in the same manner, with or without the strip lighting. This is glued into position with a special adhesive and trimmed with molding. Incidentally, with window shades, inside or ceiling brackets are used. Special side channels or stretched wires are used on large skylights, to keep them up. These are operated with a cord and pulley system.

CATHEDRAL   This is rather a difficult window to treat effectively because of its soaring proportions and the slanted windows set on the wall close to the cathedral ceiling. It is virtually impossible to hang draperies from the ceiling to the floor, as apart from being expensive, this treatment would look far too bulky with its yards and yards of fabric. Most cathedral windows are divided, just above normal door level, by a cross beam which acts as a support for the upper portions of the window. It is wisest to hang draperies from this, leaving the glass panes at ceiling level bare. Only the simplest draperies look right and you should avoid anything that is elaborate or dressy. Sheers hung from the cross beam can also be utilized and they are especially effective if the window fronts onto a good view and if privacy is not a major consideration. Window shades are the best alternative to draperies because they are tailored and sleek, and don't detract from the inherent drama of the soaring window. If you wish to shield the upper portions of the window from glare and sun, you can have window shades specially made to fit the slanting shapes. These are bottom-up shades with the top cut on an angle so that they fit the windows under the gable. You can create an attractive coordinated look with this method, and generally this total treatment costs less than draperies hung from the cross beam, as you are saving on material and the making. If privacy and light

PROBLEM: Soaring cathedral window with peak shapes at ceiling level, the whole divided by vertical and horizontal beams.

SOLUTION: Individual window shades made especially to fit the different-sized windows.

This cathedral-style window in a modern house was extremely difficult to handle because of the different sizes of the windows, the peak shapes at the top and the dividing beams. Floor-to-ceiling draperies would have been awkward to hang and too bulky in appearance; shorter draperies, hung from the crossbeam to the floor, would have left the peak windows looking bare, unfinished and unbalanced. The simplest and least expensive treatment was obviously sets of window shades, made to fit the different shapes of the top and bottom panes of glass. Chosen in ivory to blend into the elm paneling of the walls and the window beams, the lower shades roll down from the crossbeam to the floor and matching shades above roll up to the peaked ceiling. They fit perfectly into the slanting line of the roof when they are closed. Since they are translucent they filter light by day and provide privacy by night. Black cord trimming underscores the horizontal lines of the window and ceiling beams and the illuminated wall shelf. The plain shades are subtle and unobtrusive and, when opened up completely, they allow the soaring window and outside view to dominate. They are highly practical since they are simply sponged clean with a damp cloth.

control are not important, the cathedral window can be left untreated, but furniture and plants should be arranged in front of part of it, to break up the bareness of the huge expanse of glass.

PROBLEM: An angled bay, without any strong architectural elements, awkwardly positioned at one end of a wall in a small bedroom.

SOLUTION: Draperies, shades and a valance all made of the same fabric and matched to wall covering.

When a bay has no distinguishing features or strong architectural foibles to play up, the best solution is to make it a harmonious part of the total decorative look. This is what interior designer Tom Woods did with this angled bay set at one end of a small bedroom. He softened the hard lines of the bay by using floor-length tie-back draperies below a tailored valance. The window shades, hung behind the draperies, were selected for their practicality, as well as their privacy and room-darkening qualities. Shades and valance were trimmed with three rows of fringe that pick up the curry, gold and heliotrope tones of the floral fabric and matching wallpaper. The fringe gives definition and interest to the bay area. The laminated shades are made of a heat-sensitive, adhesive-coated shade cloth to which you can laminate almost any fabric simply by ironing it on. This makes them economical for those decorating on a small budget. The wallpaper which matches the fabric is also easy to put up yourself, since it is pre-pasted and only needs dipping into water to be hung. The designer completed the bay with an area rug and a table and chairs for breakfast or paperwork.

PROBLEM: Ugly Victorian bow, with strong architectural features, awkwardly positioned off-center at one end of a kitchen wall.

SOLUTION: Paint, wallpaper, combination window shades and small-scale furniture.

The architectural abnormalities of this very dominant bow in the kitchen of a Victorian house were turned to advantage by interior designer Carl Fuchs. He actually gave the difficult and awkwardly positioned window striking new looks through imaginative decorating and use of paint and wallpaper. He also cleverly utilized minimum space to the fullest by transforming the area into a dining nook. Previously wasted, the window area now gives extra livability to the kitchen. The Victorian bow, off center and set at one end of the main wall, was treated to the same green and white leaf-patterned paper used on the kitchen walls. This produces continuity. Frames and dado below the windows were painted dark green to blend with the wallpaper and also to make these architectural elements stand out as a feature of the area. Brackets and molding of the arch were painted white for contrast. Since the odd shape of the bow precluded the use of draperies, the designer selected window shades as the best alternative. He coupled pull-down and pull-up shades at each of the slim windows for an unusual combination. They provide a trim, tailored effect, privacy and the light control so essential in a kitchen. The pull-down shades are translucent and tame glare during the day. The bottom, pull-up shades are a heavier weight and are trimmed with polka-dotted green grosgrain that repeats the colors of the wall covering. A hanging plant adds to the decorative look of the nook, which is furnished with an old table and two kitchen chairs spray-painted pristine white. Apart from being the most effective treatment for the bow, it was also the most inexpensive.

27

FRENCH   The problem with this window is that it is actually a door or doors, allowing access to the outside. For this reason the treatment must be carefully selected. The main point to bear in mind is that the treatment must be one which does not get tangled with the window when it is opened or closed. It *must* be easy to manipulate for exit and entry. Full-length draperies that pull across may be used, if these are your preference and if they best suit the style of the room. However, there are several alternatives that work just as well. Vertical blinds that draw across to fit neatly at one side are ideal, as are louvered doors that fold back. You can also utilize louvered shutters providing these also fold back to allow easy use of the door. Window shades are practical since these pull up above door level and do not interfere with traffic. If you want to do something really unusual you might consider a shoji screen that slides open or a panel track with fabric that pulls back. The latter creates a striking effect, since the fabric hangs from the ceiling track in the manner of a wall hanging and is most decorative. In this instance you need sufficient wall space to the left or right of the French door, because two panels of fabric are required. When closed they hang side by side, covering both the door and a portion of the wall. When opened to allow exit and entry, the panel of fabric over the door slides behind the one covering the wall.

PICTURE   This window is difficult to decorate when it has movable sections, because the treatment must then allow for opening and clos-ing. However, whether it has these structural elements or is one single large pane of fixed glass, your prime consideration is to play up the view. Because a picture window, by nature of its size, pulls the outdoors inside, a treatment must emphasize the view and direct the eye outside. A simple treatment that frames the window is the most effective for this purpose. Draperies and a tailored valance are ideal and you can leave the actual glass bare if privacy is not a major problem. If you want to filter light and provide privacy as well, you can add light sheers or window shades. But always use sheers that easily pull back for easy opening and closing of the window's movable sections. Shades that pull up do not interfere with these elements at all.

RANCH   The chief difficulty with this window is that it is usually of poor proportion in relation to the wall. It is a wide window set high on a wall and it needs a treatment that will bring it into line with the overall dimensions of the wall and the room. Undoubtedly the best way to treat this window is to merge it into the background, so that its odd propor-tions are less apparent. You can easily do this by choosing a treatment that is color-matched to the walls. Simple sill-length draperies with a pleated heading are ideal, as are color-coordinated window shades. Understatement is the rule of thumb with this window, so avoid anything elaborate that brings the window into too much focus. It is possible to give the window extra balance by arranging suitable furniture underneath it, such as a sofa and end tables or a sofa with a library table behind it. The furniture cleverly fills out the wall space below the window and neither sill-length draperies nor shades get tangled with the furniture.

DORMER   This window is a problem because it is deeply recessed and set vertically in a gable projecting from a sloping roof. When there is no wall space on either side of the window, your best bet is to use a flat treatment that fits flush to the window. You have several alternatives. Window shades are ideal as are Austrian blinds, and you can also put up shirred curtains attached to a top and bottom rod. In the latter instance it is best to select a sheer fabric that permits light to filter into the room. When there is wall space on either side of the dormer you can use a variety of treatments and you can turn the recess into a cozy seating area through the addition of a built-in window seat or a chair. If you plan to do this then you should create a treatment that finishes at sill level, such as draperies and sheers or draperies and window shade. Color coordinate all these to walls and fabrics you have used in other parts of the room. A charming effect can be created by using the same fabric for both draperies and upholstery on the window seat or chair. If you wish, window shades can be laminated with fabric, to add total coordination and a custom-designed look. The recessed dormer is an ideal place to hang plants and they introduce color and extra decorative overtones. They should be suspended from the sloping ceiling of the dormer recess. Incidentally, as far as the style of the draperies is concerned, you can select tie-backs, ruffled curtains, Priscillas or simple straight draperies, whichever style suits your taste and the decorative look of the room as a whole. There is usually enough space in the dormer recess to add a valance, too, which creates a smooth, finished look at the window.

CLERESTORY   This window is difficult to handle because it is tall, skinny and shallow with a high sill, and it is generally out of balance in the room. This is because it is set high up on a wall, near ceiling level. However, you can solve most of its problems with one very simple treatment—the window shade. This is about the only one which is really successful for the clerestory window. A good architectural trick is to hang the shade at ceiling level, because this gives the window much-needed balance. Select a shade that blends with the colors in the room, and preferably one without a pattern. Anything patterned or too vivid in tone will make the window jump out and appear to be too prominent.

CORNER   This is actually composed of two windows of any style that come together in the corner of a room. They are difficult to decorate because of the two light exposures and the two vistas they present. The easiest way to overcome their problems is to treat them as one decorative unit. You can do this with draperies, curtains, window shades, shutters or louvers. By treating the corner windows as one single element you bring a feeling of unity and a smooth, unbroken look to the area. If you decide to use draperies, it is a good idea to hang one narrow stationary drapery in the corner between the two windows. Draperies hung at the outer edge of each window pull in to meet the central panel, creating a sleek flow of fabric when closed. When this treatment is open it allows the maximum of light to filter into the room. Because of the angled shape of the corner windows it is best to use a simple cornice or a French pleated heading as these are the easiest to fit. If you are considering window shades, examine the placement of the windows and their frames carefully before you begin decorating. For instance, if the windows are very close together and have a narrow frame, shades installed in the usual way may interfere with each other. If this is the case, one shade may be hung slightly higher than the other and a cornice used to conceal their irregularity. If the window frame is deep enough inside, you can use a footless bracket or you might consider a ceiling-hung installation.

PROBLEM: *A slanting skylight out of proportion to the slanting wall where it is positioned.*

SOLUTION: *Clever use of paint and a tailored window shade.*

This skylight window in an attic apartment was not only difficult to decorate, but because of its smallness it looked out of proportion on the sloping wall. Designer Peg Walker conquered both problems through the simple yet highly effective use of paint and a striped window shade. She painted the inside of the skylight's recess a bright tangerine and splashed the actual window frame with yellow. A wide stripe of tangerine was carried across the white wall for linear interest and to expand the window area by visual illusion. The tangerine on the inside of the recess also adds depth and so more importance to the skylight, giving it needed balance on the long wall. The yellow, white and tangerine all reappear in the multi-striped shade that easily closes for coziness or opens up to let in the sky. It is simple to maintain since it can be sponged clean. The designer selected the tailored shade, rather than an Austrian shade, for the skylight as this harmonizes better with the modern mood of the room.

OPPOSITE

PROBLEM: *Three tall, skinny windows set in a long wall.*

SOLUTION: *Heavy-weight draperies hung above windows at ceiling level and a deep, dropped valance.*

Three narrow windows, the corner one skinnier than the two in the center, seemed totally lost on this long wall of a paneled living room. To make them appear more in proportion to the long wall, heavy-weight draperies in a soft gold were used and carried up to the ceiling above the windows. This makes the windows look taller and wider and so gives them more importance. Broad tie-backs were positioned higher than usual to add even more balance and the whole wall was topped by a wide, dropped valance that introduces depth. Since the end window was very narrow only one tie-back drapery was used. To further break up the expanse of the long wall, a matching skirted table was positioned in the center, flanked on either side by floral tub chairs. The lamp, painting and tall vase of leaves add to the decorative effect of the wall.

31

PROBLEM: *A long window wall that turns the corner to become an L-shape, plus short windows that needed more importance for decorative style of the room.*

SOLUTION: *Floor-length tie-back sheers and shaped window shades.*

Shades and sheers as working partners provide a dramatic window treatment for this handsome bedroom, while offering a skillful solution to the handling of a long L-shaped window wall. Creamy yellow translucent shades are hung beneath matching floor-length curtains of a textured polyester. The softly draped tie-backs neatly and cleverly break up the long, dull expanse of glass, while maintaining a light airiness completely in keeping with the room's elegant mood. Ginger-brown velvet outlines both the shades' reverse-scallop hems and the draperies and gives definition to the expanse of creamy yellow. Note how the floor-length draperies add that much needed importance to the short windows, and are totally in harmony with the overall decorative look. Because room-darkening shades were used it was not necessary to go to the expense of lining the draperies, which considerably cut the cost of the whole window treatment. The desk and chair, plus the plant, bring additional interest along the long window wall.

PROBLEM: *A battery of small windows on a wall, set above unattractive radiators and air conditioner.*

SOLUTION: *Combination treatment of long curtains, cafes, shades and valance.*

By treating a battery of small windows along one wall as a whole, a feeling of smoothness and elegance was created. Light control and camouflage for ugly radiators and air conditioner was also introduced. For handsome architectural continuity, laminated shades were matched to the gray-and-white ticking valance and to the ticking-covered floor-to-ceiling struts which add balance without appearing to cut up wall. Long white curtains were hung at each end to soften the effect of the tailored shades and struts, while matching cafes were hung from black curtain rings on a brass rod. They cross the window wall to conceal the radiators and air conditioner. This highly effective combination was carried out in light neutral tones to serve as an unobtrusive background for a mixture of French, Colonial and contemporary furniture that adds up to a charming eclectic mbod. The ceiling-hung plants are decorative and colorful in front of the windows. Note how the unbroken line of the deep valance and the side curtains help to "frame" the windows and so the impression of one long window is given. The cafe curtains underscore this feeling.

WALL OF GLASS   The main problem with this window is its size and the huge expanse of glass which has to be treated. Obviously, decorating it can be extremely difficult. Usually the best way to handle this window is to play it down by using a sleek, understated treatment. Anything elaborate will make the window too prominent in the overall decor of the room. You also have to consider the view and whether or not you want to pull the outdoors inside. If the view is spectacular, select a simple treatment that does not block it out, such as tailored floor-to-ceiling draperies that frame the window. When privacy is a consideration you can add sheers, which do not obscure the outside vista totally yet limit inward vision from the outside. A poor view from an oversized window of this nature can be completely hidden by a clever treatment. Wall-to-wall transversing draperies in a sheer fabric let in light but are opaque enough to obliterate the ugly view. As an alternative, you can use floor-to-ceiling vertical blinds which run the entire length of the wall. These rotate to permit light to enter yet they stop the eye and also mask the poor vista. As always, the adaptable window shade works well on a wall of glass. But in this instance you must use a series of shades to cover the total area. You might also consider utilizing cafe curtains hung on a rod, which cut across the middle of the window and partially obscure a poor outlook. This treatment is particularly good in rooms short on wall space, as the cafe-curtained part of the window makes a suitable backdrop for furniture.

TOO SMALL/TOO LARGE   The problem with these windows is not so much their actual size, but their size in relation to the room. Because they are out of proportion with the overall dimensions they give the room an unbalanced look. The window that is too small for the room must be given a cleverly-scaled treatment that brings it into line and makes it more important looking. A window that is too large for the room should be decorated with a light-scaled treatment that plays the window down and makes it appear less prominent. You can make a window grow in stature through a few clever decorative tricks. For instance, any window will seem that much larger if you extend the treatment out onto the walls at each side and above. Draperies, shutters, shoji screens and panel tracks with fabric all produce the desired effect. When you are using draperies you can introduce even more importance with a valance or a jabot at the top.

A lambrequin that surrounds the window also helps to give it more height, width and dimension. A lambrequin is easy to make from light wood and consists of two pieces running down each side of the window to the floor and a third piece across the top. This "frame" can be painted to match the walls or covered with wallpaper or fabric and it adds decoratively to the look of the room as a whole.

Similar visual tricks help to play down the large window. For example, draperies or window shades in the same color as the walls make a window blend unobtrusively into the background. Vertical blinds, because they are tailored and sleek, work well against a large window and help to marry it with the walls. Whenever possible try to use pale colors at a large window. Light tones recede and appear to push walls and windows outwards; darker colors advance and pull the walls and window inwards, making both seem much more prominent.

AWKWARDLY POSITIONED   The problem to be overcome here is the placement of the window on a given wall. An awkwardly positioned window may be too high, too low, too close to an architectural element such as a door, a staircase or a fireplace. The oddly placed window produces an unbalanced look and the trick of course is to give it that required balance in relation to the rest of the room. When a window is set too high on a wall you can easily pull it down by visual illusion. You do this by extending the treatment below sill level, so that the window seems nearer the floor. Shutters that cover a portion of the wall below the window or floor-length draperies accomplish this, as does a panel track with fabric which drops below the window level. A series of narrow shelves built underneath the window adds a feeling of extra length, or you can place a small table in this spot for the same effect. When plants are used on either you create a charming garden look that at once enhances the room as well as the window area.

The window that is set too low on the wall has to be made to seem taller, and again you can do this with some visual tricks. The idea here is to extend the window upwards towards the ceiling. Shutters that go higher than the window are ideal, as is a panel track set on the ceiling with fabric falling down to cover the portion of wall above the low window. Window shades can be installed at ceiling level to bring the window into line effectively. If you want to utilize draperies, extend them higher than the window and add a deep valance to cover part of the wall area immediately above the window.

When a window is set too close to an architectural element, it has to be treated as simply as possible, so that it does not compete with that element. Plain window shades are your best solution.

ADJOINING   These windows are usually set too close together and present a problem because they are hard to decorate individually. If you give each window a separate treatment you create a busy, cluttered look. The best solution is to treat the adjoining windows as one unit, in much the same way you would treat corner windows. You can produce a smooth, flowing feeling by utilizing matching window shades interspersed with tie-back draperies; tie-back draperies and sheers; or a series of shutters or vertical blinds.

VIEWLESS   When a window looks out onto no view at all or an unattractive one, it presents certain problems. Simply covering up the window entirely is not always a good solution, especially when you need light and air in the room. However, you can create treatments that stop the eye and which also allow the circulation of light and air. These include translucent shoji screens, Austrian blinds, vertical blinds, louvered shutters and opaque sheers framed by side draperies. Cafe curtains can be utilized to mask a poor view and these work extremely well in combination with translucent window shades. One interior designer I knew created a charming effect in a window area which looked out onto a miserable view. She attached a series of narrow glass shelves across the front of the window and then filled the shelves with plants. A simple lambrequin gave the window the necessary finishing touch. The plants cleverly obscured the poor view yet allowed light to permeate the room. The window could also be opened when required. Decorative glass objects could be used on the shelves instead of, or along with, plants, for a different look.

When light is not a major consideration you can utilize sliding panels or free-standing screens decorated with paint, fabric or a wall covering. Mirrored screens are effective and, of course, a panel track and fabric also help to solve this particular problem.

WRONG STYLE   This type of window is usually in line with the architectural feeling of the room but wrong for the actual decorative style you are going to introduce with furniture. For example, a modern window does not work well with a traditional look, while an old-fashioned window is obviously out of place with modern decor.

Since a period-style room usually demands traditional draperies, your best bet is first to mask the modern window with simple sheers or a plain window shade. You can then go ahead and treat the window to handsome draperies and a fancy valance, since the sheers or shades won't compete. If your preference is for a structural treatment, such as shutters or louvers, you must again first mask the modern window with simple window shades.

When you are giving an old-fashioned room a modern look with modern furniture, you will have to update the old-fashioned window with an appropriate treatment. Obviously this is much less costly than making structural changes to the window itself. The best treatments to use with modern decor are vertical blinds; floor-to-ceiling draperies, tailored in style with a plain French heading; window shades; and panel tracks with fabric. Fortunately, most of these treatments successfully hide the whole window and so you do not necessarily need to add a masking treatment as well.

For example, if you are using floor-to-ceiling draperies, select a lightweight fabric which permits light to filter into the room. By using such a fabric you will be able to keep the draperies closed for a sleek background, while hiding the old-fashioned window at the same time. Vertical blinds running floor to ceiling across a window cleverly conceal its architectural style, and by rotating the vanes you get sufficient light without revealing too much of the window itself. If you decide to utilize a panel track select a translucent fabric, again to permit light to enter. You can then keep the panels of fabric permanently closed. Shoji screens with translucent panels work in a similar way.

PRACTICAL TIPS

Easy maintenance is an important consideration when you are selecting a window treatment. Before finally deciding on a particular treatment, think of it in terms of upkeep so that you can determine whether or not it is practical for you. Remember that all elaborate or fussy decorative treatments collect dust and are more difficult to clean than those that are strictly tailored and simple.

Always look for materials that are easy to keep up and which won't cost you a fortune to dry-clean. In fact, whenever possible select fabrics that you can easily wash yourself, either by hand or in the washing machine. Window shades are extremely practical since they are relatively simple to clean by dusting or with a damp sponge. Structural treatments such as louvers, shutters, shoji screens, sliding panels and screens are equally practical and clean in the same manner as window shades. Vertical blinds made of shade cloth can be kept pristine by regular dusting and occasional damp-sponging. The fabric used with a panel track can be removed easily and either dry-cleaned or washed at home. However, you can keep this relatively clean by regularly running the brush attachment of the vacuum over it, and so limit washing or cleaning to once a year.

PROBLEM: *Small, double-hung window, old-fashioned in design and awkwardly positioned at one end of a bathroom wall.*

SOLUTION: *Combination of shade, shutters and matching valance.*

In the able hands of interior designer Ann Heller this odd little window gained new decorative importance and fresh good looks. After the bathroom had been streamlined through a remodeling job, the old-fashioned window looked out of place; also, its awkward placement between the large mirror and the bath area made it hard to decorate. For instance, this positioning precluded the use of curtains. The designer created a charming combination treatment that fits neatly into the window frame yet has color, pattern and design interest. It also provides privacy as well as camouflage for the ugly window. She used a spare roll of wallpaper, left over from the ceiling, to cover a simple valance easily made from a piece of light plywood. The lively patchwork pattern of bright pink, red, orange, yellow and white creates an interesting change of pace as it transfers from the valance to the fabric-covered shade done with a do-it-yourself method of press-on lamination. Below, open shutters were fitted with the same amusing print, shirred into place. The shutters were painted a cheerful yellow to match the other woodwork in the bathroom.

PROBLEM: *A medium-sized picture window placed off-center on a long wall. Already decorated with vertical blinds, the window needed to be given a finished look and more importance for the scale of the room.*

SOLUTION: *A lambrequin covered with an attractive fabric.*

Vertical blinds were used to cloak this picture window, positioned off-center on a living room wall. The blinds gave much needed balance to the awkwardly placed window, which cut into the wall and did not run floor-to-ceiling. By running the blinds up to the ceiling and extending them at the sides, the

window was brought into line. However, it did not gain enough importance for the scale of the room and it looked unfinished. Designer Michael Sherman corrected this by adding a lambrequin around the window. This at once added the necessary finishing touch by creating a "frame" effect for the white-shade-cloth verticals. It also produced a more important-looking window in a better scale for the size of the room. The designer preferred to use the lambrequin instead of draperies, as this underscores the tailored look of the verticals and is harmonious with the modern mood of the room. The lambrequin was made of light plywood and covered with the green and yellow floral fabric. It also cost much less than draperies.

PROBLEM: Two old-fashioned windows set close together on a small wall, with a protruding radiator set in between them.

SOLUTION: Short, shaped lambrequins, cafe curtains and window shades.

This pair of small, old-fashioned windows was difficult to decorate effectively because of their closeness to each other, the smallness of the wall and the awkwardly placed radiator set between them. It was not feasible to use full-length draperies at each window because the protruding radiator would have prevented easy flow of the fabric; short, sill-length curtains were also dismissed as they would have been too unimportant in appearance. Designer Pete Cano's solution was this unusual treatment which stems from the facile use of curved lambrequins, printed cafe curtains and solid-color window shades. The designer stayed within the windows' narrow perimeters yet created design interest and handsome looks without sacrificing practicality. The short cafe curtains are softly draped and so effectively balance the tailored look of the shades and lambrequins. Equally as important, they do not interfere with the radiator on the center of the wall. The lambrequins help to make each window look slightly larger, as do the cafe rods, which hardly infringe on the wall space. The curtains in a fruit pattern and the plaid lambrequins are color-coordinated in shades of putty and navy blue; delphinium blue window shades make a harmonious blend. Lights hidden behind the lambrequins give dramatic emphasis to the windows. When extra daylight is required, shades roll up easily and cafe curtains are drawn back.

2 · Decorating Awkwardly Shaped Rooms

The easiest rooms to decorate are those which are beautifully proportioned and which have no architectural oddities to throw them off balance.

Of course not every room has these perfect, well-scaled proportions; in fact, by and large, the majority of rooms in most homes are awkwardly shaped or have built-in defects and so they seem problematical to decorate and furnish well.

Typical oddly shaped rooms found in both apartments and houses include those that are long and narrow, small and squat, oddly angled, large and barnlike or with ceilings that are too high or too low. Then there are rooms with built-in architectural defects, such as alcoves, niches, badly placed windows, an off-center fireplace or awkward staircase. Sometimes a room has too many doors and this can also create a decorating problem.

Essentially, all these peculiarities break up the smooth flow of wall space, making it difficult to arrange furniture easily for the ultimate in comfort and looks. Often they give the room an unbalanced look. Yet even the most awkwardly-shaped room has the potential to live well and a little skillful decorating helps it to live up to its potential. Often the odd shapes and architectural defects can be turned to advantage, so that they add a certain degree of charm and uniqueness to the overall decorative scheme. In fact, I have sometimes found these rooms much more interesting to decorate than those that are perfectly square and well-proportioned, because they have real character and lend themselves to interesting effects.

The problems inherent in awkwardly shaped rooms can be solved through camouflage and visual illusion, which is much easier and cheaper than going to the expense of making involved structural changes. The clever use of color, wall coverings, floor coverings and the

41

strategic placement and arrangement of furniture help you to disguise and deflect the eye from the oddities extremely well. However, before you start the actual decorating, it is a good idea to have an overall plan for the room down on paper. Carefully thought-out plans make decorating all that much easier, and they save time and money since they prevent you from making mistakes.

Before you start thinking about color schemes, fabrics, wall and floor coverings and camouflaging or visual tricks, it is vitally important to make a floor plan of the room. This is an essential tool in decorating and it is not complicated to make. You should first measure the room and jot down the height, width and length in a notebook. Measure the doors, windows, alcoves and any other architectural oddities as well. Once you have all these essential measurements in feet translate them to a workable size, using the scale of half an inch equals one foot or one inch equals one foot, whichever you find easier to handle. Draw the outline of the room on graph paper or plain, unlined paper, and be sure to indicate such things as windows, doors and any other architectural elements that are prominent, such as alcoves, niches, wall jogs, protruding wall beams, a fireplace or staircase. If any of the walls are angled or oddly shaped, be sure to indicate this, too. The floor plan you have made will clarify the room's overall dimensions visually and, since it pinpoints all the peculiarities as well, you will have a better idea of the basic problems you have to overcome. Apart from this, a floor plan helps you to ascertain just how much furniture you can comfortably include in a room, showing you what it might be necessary to discard if you are redecorating or what you should buy if you are decorating from scratch. The floor plan will also tell you where to create a focal point, if a natural one does not exist. Once you have decided on the amount of furniture you can easily include for comfort and good looks, you can create miniature furniture arrangements on the plan. The easiest way to do this is to lightly sketch them in with pencil, erasing ones which do not work. Some people prefer to use templates. These are small cut-outs of the various pieces of furniture, made from colored paper and drawn to the exact scale. Remember, arranging furniture on paper is much easier than doing it physically. Make as many furniture groupings as you wish, until you find the one which suits the room, its functions and your living needs.

When you have completed your floor plan you can consider the color schemes you like and which you think will work best in the room. Color is one of the most important elements in an awkwardly shaped room. This is because it is a unifier which blends furnishings and seemingly unrelated objects together for a cohesive, balanced whole. It can also be used to hide architectural oddities and change a room's dimensions. For instance, certain colors expand the size of a small room, and others introduce coziness and intimacy into a more spacious one, through visual illusion.

While you are planning your color scheme you should give some thought to all the types of wall coverings available today. Some of them are especially ideal for camouflaging poor architectural elements, such as wood paneling, fabrics and vinyl that simulates suede or leather. Others help to expand space visually, in particular mirrored panels and mirrored tiles, sheets of copper or chrome and wallpapers that have an airy, open pattern.

Certain floor coverings can produce similar visual tricks in a room and they should be carefully coordinated to the wall covering used. For example, a light-colored, unpatterned wall-to-wall flooring material such as carpet or vinyl tile seems to expand the floor area; a dark, patterned wall-to-wall floor covering will reduce the feeling of spaciousness considerably. Area rugs and carpets can also reduce the feeling of spaciousness, because they break up the flow of space. Yet in some instances these can be cleverly utilized to pull seating arrangements together and to define specific areas within the room. A well-thought-out floor treatment can work wonders in an awkwardly shaped room. It can either unify odd alcoves and niches with the rest of the room or distract the eye from peculiarly angled walls.

SOLUTIONS FOR TYPICAL AWKWARD SHAPES

Obviously there are all kinds of awkwardly shaped rooms and it is not possible to pinpoint every one of them in this book. However, there are about a dozen awkward shapes that are typical in many homes and these are the ones you are most likely to come across. They are listed here along with some simple and inexpensive solutions, which are also relatively easy to create yourself.

LONG AND NARROW   You would be surprised at the number of skinny rooms there are and most people who are faced with them are at a loss to know how to decorate them effectively. If you have a long skinny room, don't despair. There are several ways you can bring it into line so that it looks attractive and functions comfortably.

Obviously the problem with this room is its elongated, corridor-like shape. It literally seems to defy good decoration because it lacks the usual squared-off proportions and width. It is costly to give it well-scaled dimensions through structural changes and often it is not even feasible to attempt this. But you can solve its problems by visual illusion. Through the ingenious use of materials and color you can make it appear squarer and wider than it really is and certain well-arranged furniture groupings will help to underscore this effect.

The long, narrow room is composed of a short wall at each end, plus two longer side walls. The scale of this kind of room is totally unbalanced because of the discrepancies in the actual lengths of the walls. The basic idea is to make the room look less elongated, wider and squarer in shape. There are several solutions.

Color The right colors will work magic in the long, narrow room. The trick is to use two different colors which strongly contrast with each other. A dark or vivid shade should be utilized on the short end walls to pull them in towards the center; a light or pale color must then be used on the long side walls to push them out for a feeling of extra width. This combination produces a much more balanced look in the room, by illusion of course. Good colors to use on the end walls are brown, red, fir green, deep blue, purple and orange. All of these strong colors appear to advance into the room. Suitable colors to use on the long side walls include white, sand, beige, mushroom, pale gray and light pastels, depending on the colors on the end walls. All pale or light colors recede and appear to push walls out.

Here are some suggested combinations that work together most successfully to create the desired squarer look. All the dark colors go on the short end walls, of course, the lighter tones on the side walls.

Brown with beige, sand, mushroom or soft coral. *Red* with white, beige, sand or mushroom. *Fir Green* with pale apple green or white. *Blue* with pale sky blue or white. *Purple* with pale gray, lemon or white. *Orange* with white, sand, beige or lemon.

PROBLEM: *Long wall with an old-fashioned fireplace, arched doorless entrance from hall, arched niche too close to protruding corner columns and ceiling beam cutting across the wall.*

SOLUTION: *Removal of mantelshelf, remodeling of arched doorway and niche and a total new facade with paneling.*

Although the owner of this apartment liked the spa-

ciousness of the living room he was dismayed by the old-fashioned fireplace wall and the other architectural defects, such as the unattractive arched niche and protruding columns in the corner. He also wanted to reduce the barren feeling of the room.

Interior designer Virginia Frankel took on the task of totally remodeling the long, awkward wall to give it more flowing dimensions and a contemporary look compatible with the owner's taste in furnishings. She began by removing the mantelshelf over the fireplace and tearing out the bookshelves and the bottom cupboard in the niche. Both the arched niche and the arched doorway were squared off for a neat, tailored appearance. The niche was transformed into a roomy storage closet and given doors that fit flush with the adjoining walls. When closed they are hardly visible and do not disrupt the smooth expanse of space introduced by the paneling. This was carried up to the ceiling to mask the long ceiling beam cutting across the wall. Old-English-elm plywood paneling has a hardwood finish and a random-planked look. The light tones and the vertical lines of the paneling help to give additional height to the long wall; the textural effect introduces needed warmth in the large room. To balance the small fireplace, the designer hung a large metal sculpture off-center on the wall and backed this up with tall plants and a brass floor lamp with a black shade. Positioning of the checked wing chair, ottoman and old chest further underscores the balance of the wall. The craftsman panels are produced in 4′ x 7′ and 8′ x 10′ lengths and all are a quarter of an inch thick. They are easy to put up and unfinished edges are concealed by matching floor and ceiling molding.

PROBLEM: A small second bedroom which had to function on three different levels; need to visually expand confined dimensions.

SOLUTION: Use of built-ins and a sofa bed; light-toned paneling; pale draperies and carpet.

Space problems can be overcome through good planning and skillful use of materials and color. These are the techniques I used when I turned a small extra bedroom in our New York apartment into a library-office-guest room. I made the one room function as three. Four elements were vital to make the room function on these various levels. These were a large-sized desk for writing; storage space for stationery and files; plenty of bookshelves; and a comfortable sleep sofa for the occasional overnight guest. It was also important that the room function well after working hours, as a library-sitting room for family relaxation and entertaining. Since the room was relatively small and somewhat narrow, it was necessary to plan all these elements carefully to get the most out of the available space. Color and materials had to be used effectively to create the illusion of more space than there really was. To solve the problem of storage space for various items and books, I designed a long wall of shelves and cupboards with a counter top in the center. This holds the TV set and serves as a small bar. By running the built-in unit the length of the longest wall and taking it right up to the ceiling level, everything was housed. The built-in was made of wood and then faced with plywood paneling in a light birch tone. The central portion of the wall above the counter was painted royal blue for a change of pace and to add a flash of bright color. The blue is accented by the old English prints of knights in armor which are matted in red. The window wall at the end of the room was treated to floor-length white textured draperies which add a feeling of extra height and lightness in the room. White nylon carpeting was put down on the floor to further the illusion of spaciousness underfoot. Two modern armless chairs were used because their white pedestal bases give them a "floating" look and they take up little space. They are easy to move and swivel around for TV viewing.

For continuity with the bookshelf-storage wall, the rest of the room was also covered with the same light-colored birch paneling. This not only adds depth and dimension but pushes walls out so that the confined, narrow room appears to be twice as large. Vertical ridges in the paneling introduce a feeling of height, as does the red white and blue wall hanging. This is made of two panels of fabric, hung on panel tracks, and it hides a third window in the room; it simply pulls open to reveal the window. The desk and typing table are also built-ins which I had built to my own specifications. They create an L-shape at one end of the room, which is totally self-contained for working. Their straight lines maintain the sleek, uncluttered look of the room. Made of sturdy wood, they were covered with a plastic laminate that has the look of butcher-block wood. The sand tones of this high-pressure plastic laminate blend well with the color of the paneling. To utilize space to the fullest, a sleep sofa was chosen in place of an ordinary sofa. This provides total seating comfort during the day, but opens up into a queen-sized bed, when required for the occasional guest. The light sand suede upholstery is actually a man-made vinyl, chosen because it blends well with the color scheme and is also hard-wearing. The blue-skirted table next to the sleep sofa is actually a metal filing cabinet with the addition of a circular wood top; a circular glass top protects the cloth and adds wipe-clean practicality. It houses extra papers and files not contained in the base cupboards of the built-in bookshelf unit. Apart from functioning on many levels, the room is highly practical to maintain. Paneling simply dusts clean, while desk and typing table sponge down with soap and water. The nylon carpet and vinyl upholstery on the sofa are soil-resistant and spot-clean with ease.

Patterns Certain patterned wall coverings work in much the same way as strong colors if you put them on the end walls. When the patterns are large scaled, strong and vividly colored they tend to advance into a room. Any of these types of patterned wall coverings can be successfully used on end walls to pull them forward, but it is wise to restrict the wall covering to the end walls *only*, otherwise you will defeat your purpose. Side walls should be painted in a light color that is harmonious with one of the softer colors in the wall covering itself. Some wall coverings have coordinated mates that have similar but diffused, softer patterns and in this instance you can use the two together. For example, you can get a trellis-and-floral pattern that matches up with a plain trellis design; a stripes-and-floral pattern that teams with plain stripes. There are many such combinations available. All airy patterns tend to open up walls and are ideal to use on side walls of a long, narrow room, since they introduce that much-needed balance.

Reflective materials Wall coverings that have a reflective quality are good to use in skinny rooms, because they lead the eye out and so help to create a feeling of added depth. These include mirrored panels and tiles, panels of copper or chrome, and all wallpapers with a metallic background such as the silver and copper Mylars. These materials create a three-dimensional look as they push the walls out and introduce depth through their seeming infinity. They should be used on one or both of the long side walls in combination with dark colors or a patterned wall covering on the short end walls. When using mirror always be sure it has something interesting to reflect, otherwise it misses out on its potential. For instance, when it shows images of a major seating arrangement, paintings and accessories you get a real feeling of extra dimension which naturally adds balance in the room. The reflections which show up in copper and chrome panels are more diffused, but nevertheless it is still better for them to reflect objects rather than a blank wall. Mylar-type wallpapers don't have exactly the same reflective qualities, but since they both push walls out and bounce light back into the room they too introduce width.

Furniture A really well arranged and well positioned furniture grouping does a great deal to underscore the effects created by cleverly handled walls. For example, a major seating grouping arranged in an open, airy shape in the center of the room produces balance. The arrangement might be square, L-shaped, U-shaped or semicircular, depending on the size of the room and your personal tastes and living needs. The grouping can be composed of one or two sofas, several chairs, a coffee table and lamp tables, but whatever pieces you use, be sure the arrangement is strong and dominant so that it acts as a center of gravity. The short end walls can then be treated accordingly. If these short end walls are not broken up by windows and doors, you will be able to utilize large pieces of furniture here, perhaps an armoire, an etagere, a piano or bookcases. Dominant pieces of furniture appear to advance into the room and so seem to pull the short walls closer to the center. If one of the end walls does have a window, give it a fairly dominant treatment to pull it forward.

Interior designer Joan Blutter has several tried and tested furniture arrangements which work well against end walls and help to pull them into the room, producing better proportion throughout. She calls them her "standard formulas" and certainly they do much to counteract the long, corridor-like look. None of them is difficult to create.

She often uses a secondary seating arrangement against an end wall, smaller in size than the major central arrangement. It is composed of a Parsons table or library table, a love seat or small sofa and a coffee table. Joan positions the Parsons or library table about nine inches away from the short end wall and places the love seat or small sofa immediately in front of this, with the back of the sofa flush with the edge of the table. The coffee table goes in front of the sofa.

The table behind the love seat is utilized for fairly dominant accessories, such as a lamp, tall plants or accessories; if she has the available space the designer adds an end table at one end of the sofa and two handsome stools or ottomans at the other side of the coffee table facing the love seat. When the space is confined she might replace the end table with a tall plant, a pedestal holding sculpture, a tall floor lamp if she is not using a lamp on the table. This staggered arrangement of pieces of furniture advances into the room, pulling in the end walls for that squarer look required to make a skinny room look all that much better.

When a secondary seating arrangement is not appropriate, Joan has another of her "standards" as an alternate. This is composed of a desk, a desk chair and a tall plant. Joan positions the desk chair about two or three feet away from the end wall, facing into the room. The desk goes in front of this, also facing into the room, with the tall plant in a corner to one side. Once again, the end wall is pulled forward for the desired effect.

Yet a third "standard" is a library wall. Joan covers the entire end wall with floor-to-ceiling bookshelves and fills them with plants and accessories as well as books. A chair and an ottoman facing into the room, plus a small table for a lamp, or a floor lamp, round out the grouping, which also appears to move forward into the room.

Joan Blutter suggests treating the opposite end wall to a large piece of furniture, such as an etagere, a baker's rack or a handsome screen; if possible the latter should be highlighted by a floor lamp and a tall plant or a collection of plants.

Floor coverings All patterned floor coverings tend to reduce the feeling of space in a long, narrow room, so that the length seems to be less obvious. Some patterned flooring materials can be used cleverly to introduce a feeling of width by visual illusion, in particular horizontal-striped patterns, as well as florals and geometrics which run horizontally across the floor covering. Squares in contrasting colors, plaids, tartans and cubic designs also help to visually expand narrow areas, for like stripes they lead the eye across rather than down. Look for all of these patterns in both carpets and vinyl tiles. Area rugs and carpets break up the flow of space and can also be utilized to suggest extra width. For example, a large area rug in the center of the room introduces a squared-off look on this part of the floor and is ideal for pulling a large central seating arrangement together. Floor space at either end of the room which is not covered by the area rug should be given good secondary furniture arrangements or a dominant piece of furniture. They help to fill out the space and counteract the isolation of floor areas at each end.

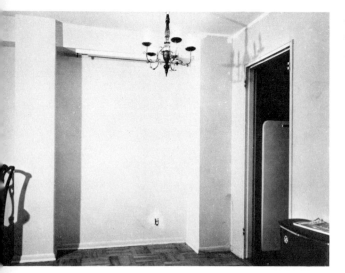

PROBLEM: *Two vertical columns and a horizontal ceiling beam that broke up the flow of the main wall in a dining room. They created useless adjoining alcoves too small to decorate effectively. Two doors cut up the second wall.*

SOLUTION: *Paneling and built-in cabinet and bookshelves.*

Architectural defects in this dining room of an old-fashioned city apartment made it seem hopeless to decorate. One wall was cut up by awkward columns and a beam; another by two doors. This meant there was no real unbroken wall space against which furniture could be arranged.

The whole room was sheathed in paneling to bring all the architectural problems into line and create a smooth, flowing look. The ceiling beam above the larger alcove was built out to align with the columns and to become a light box. The columns thus seem less apparent and the plywood paneling makes the small room grow visually because of its light sable and beige tones and sleek surface. Although the main alcove was too small for a piece of furniture it did accommodate the slender built-in cabinet which provides storage space and a display surface for a collection of crystal accessories. The dropped light box, faced with translucent glass, provides illumination in this area and highlights the painting. Dead space in the second alcove was treated to bookshelves and utilized for handsome oversized volumes. New double-hung doors were covered with matching paneling so that they become less obvious through their harmony with the walls. The room takes on a whole new appearance through the use of the paneling, which is practical and economical since it is simple to clean by regularly dusting and it wears well for years. Because of its long life span it dispenses with the need for continual repainting; added boons are its insulation and soundproofing qualities.

PROBLEM: *Awkwardly positioned, off-center fireplace, open stairs, continuing wall on other side of stairs.*

SOLUTION: *Paneling, white paint, wall-to-wall carpet plus clever furniture arrangement and use of accessories.*

Odd placement of fireplace close to the stairs created a real decorating problem in this basement being remodeled into a family room. Interior designer Ving Smith knew it was not possible, for practical reasons, to move the fireplace. So instead he created a sense of balance through the clever use of materials and a few inspired visual tricks. His theory was to pull the eyes away from the right wall and the open stairs toward the fireplace and the left of the room. To accomplish this he had to make the fireplace wall the most dominant in the room. To this end he covered the fireplace wall with paneling using a horizontal lap design; the fireplace itself was painted bright white. For continuity in the room the designer masked the right wall with matching paneling, but hung it vertically so that it is much less dominant. Both walls are linked by the wide beam. He used green wall-to-wall carpet throughout, carrying it up the stairs, again for flowing continuity. The stairs are at once integrated into the room and are therefore not so obvious. With the shell in place, the designer then set about arranging the furniture for the best effect. His anchor was the white area rug in front of the fireplace. The sofa and chair, plus end tables, were grouped around this immediately in line with the fireplace. A white Parsons table behind the chair also helps to add definition to the grouping. Finally, to further pull the eye away from the stairs, Ving Smith placed the most dominant accessories to the left of the fireplace. These include the two oil paintings, the lamp and a plant in the corner of the room. Such visual tricks are ideal to use when it is either too costly or too difficult to rebuild or alter poor architectural elements. His decision not to put a door at the bottom of the stairs was based on the narrowness of the opening and the inconvenience of a door swinging into the living room so close to the fireplace.

LARGE & BARNLIKE   Although spaciousness is a boon in most homes, a room of really soaring proportions can often seem overly cold and uninviting. Even when you have plenty of furniture in the room this feeling may persist. However, it can be counteracted by clever use of color, wall coverings, floor coverings and furniture arrangements.

All of these elements can be utilized to reduce the cold, barren look by introducing warmth and intimacy, without any loss of actual physical space.

Color   Your first priority is to select a color scheme. Pale colors have built-in coolness that only serves to emphasize the barnlike proportions. They not only recede and push walls out but reflect light and bounce it back into the room. It is obviously wiser to avoid using these. Consider instead some of the darker, warmer or more vivid shades, which all advance into the room and so help to make it seem smaller than it really is. Red, brown, peach, dark green and olive green, deep blue, rose, vivid yellow and terra cotta are all ideal because they pull the walls in and so introduce intimacy. A high ceiling, painted white, often furthers the barren look but this can be lowered, by visual illusion of course, if you paint it to match the walls or in a tone slightly lighter than the walls. Interior designer Michael Greer always uses this technique in rooms that are overly large, because he feels white is too stark a contrast with colored walls and visually pushes the ceiling upward.

Wall coverings   If you don't want to use paint on the walls, there are a variety of different wall coverings you can consider and which help to alleviate the coldness created by barnlike proportions. Wood paneling, fabrics, and suede- and leather-like vinyls are most successful in these rooms because they introduce textural interest as well as color. Wallpapers are also effective, in particular strong or large-scaled patterns. As I pointed out earlier, all patterns tend to advance and so reduce the overall dimensions. They also effectively break up the flow of wall space and of course bring lots of lively color interest into the room. Avoid minute patterns in a large room, which are out of scale with the soaring proportions and only emphasize them.

Floor coverings   Soft floor coverings, such as wall-to-wall carpeting, area rugs and carpets, are the best kind to use in a very large room, as they introduce texture, color and warmth. The cold overtones are diminished most effectively by rich, dark or vivid colors. Pale tones only help to promote the feeling of great space. Hard floors, such as wood, and resilient floor coverings like vinyl, also tend to emphasize the barren feeling, so it is better to avoid using them. If they already exist in a large room, partially cover them with area rugs or carpets, as these will add

53

that necessary texture, color and warmth. They also visually break up the flow of the floor space for a cozier look.

Furniture Well-planned furniture arrangements do much to bring a large room into decorative line, because they fill up the space in the most pleasing manner. The most appropriate to use are groupings that are airy and open; small, tight arrangements will look out of proportion in the vast expanse of space. Some large pieces of furniture are needed to introduce a balanced look, but do not overdo this or you will create a top-heavy feeling. Choose a tall etagere, a piano, an armoire or bookcases, but do not include all of them. If you want to use two large pieces in a room, be sure they are not placed too close together. Sofas and chairs should be relatively large in size and coffee tables and end tables should be of a scale that blends with these. Avoid using lots of small pieces of furniture; apart from looking lost, they promote an overly cluttered look and a furniture-showroom ambiance. Pay special attention to lighting in a large room. Lamps should be handsome and of a good size, again for proportion and balance; they should also be strategically placed around the room to distribute light evenly. Mirrors, paintings, prints and any other wall accessories should also be relatively large, so they do not look lost on the large walls.

Interior designer Jane Victor firmly believes in using at least three seating arrangements in a large room. These do not necessarily have to be all major seating groupings; she suggests creating one central arrangement, balanced by smaller, secondary arrangements at either end of the room. She then fills up the wall space in between with several large pieces, perhaps a piano balanced by an armoire or an etagere in another area. This formula evenly breaks up the grand flow of space and also helps the room to function well for living needs. She always designs a strong or dominant window treatment for this kind of room; if the window or windows are relatively small in proportion to the room she utilizes a treatment that extends out onto the adjoining walls for better scale.

PROBLEM: *Large zigzag-shaped hallway at the top of a staircase with wasted space under the window.*

SOLUTION: *Built-in storage and new carpeting.*

This large hallway at the top of the staircase in a suburban house was totally wasted space, mainly because of its peculiar shape. The landing leading to the children's bedrooms was an odd zigzag shape and difficult to handle. So was the area under a sloping ceiling next to a recessed window. Deciding what to

do with the area to make it more useful was the baffling problem until the owners decided to turn it into a children's storage and play area. In effect it became a practical extension of their rooms. A long, low storage unit composed of drawers and cupboards was built along the window wall to make the most use of this awkwardly angled area. Shelves were added on top of the storage unit, cleverly built in to fit neatly under the sloping roof. A large wooden box, covered with colorful floral paper and fitted with a lock, was placed against the shorter side wall and became the base for a set of light-weight wooden shelves that neatly store other toys. It also doubles as a roomy storage chest for winter clothes. New bright-red shag carpeting was put down, mainly to muffle noise and cushion tumbles, but it also adds a cheerful note to the area. When the children outgrow the toys, the storage easily converts into bookshelves and can be used for more adult items.

No kid-glove treatment is needed for the carpet made of 100 percent nylon; it cleans up readily after the stickiest spills. Woodwork also wipes clean with ease.

55

PROBLEM: Oddly shaped, cramped hallway badly cut into by two doors and opening directly into the living room.

SOLUTION: Cleverly designed floor, use of white paint, one dominant piece of furniture and plants.

Apart from its odd shape and the multitude of doors which cut it up visually, this hallway had another basic problem. It opened directly into the living room and because there was no door it was easily visible from there. This same "overview" effect was carried through into the kitchen when the door was open. It was also cramped and dreary.

Interior designer Virginia Frankel solved the main problem in this hallway through a skillful visual trick. By carrying a section of the living room floor covering on into the hallway she created a feeling of integration between the two areas. The pie-shaped wedge of white vinyl leads the eye both in and out of the hallway for an illusion of extended space. To create the same flowing effect between the kitchen and the hall, she ran the patterned kitchen vinyl into hall also. Placed on either side of the white wedge it too expands the spacious look, because once again it pulls the eye beyond the perimeter of the hall. With the floor in place, the designer then set about decorating the hallway. To play down the doors she painted them the same white as the walls so that they virtually disappear. The same white lacquer splashes up onto the ceiling and its light tone and reflective quality counteract the dreary, dark mood. The treatment of the walls and floor overcomes the cramped appearance of the hall, so that it is opened up considerably. Rather than filling the hall with small pieces of furniture which would have introduced a cluttered look, the designer selected one large piece. This is a handsome antique armoire, which becomes a dramatic accent. Because it is so highly visual and dominant it too helps to distract the eye away from the hall's defects. A large potted plant cleverly bridges the awkward space between two door jambs and along with other plants adds a decorative touch. The green and white color scheme of the hall blends well with the yellow and white scheme that predominates in the living room.

PROBLEM: *A large landing at the top of a staircase with an oddly angled corner, sloping ceiling, no side walls and long, narrow dimensions.*

SOLUTION: *Paint, patterned carpet, tailored furniture that is cleverly grouped.*

This landing, lost space at the top of a house, went to waste for a long time until it was retrieved and turned into a comfortable extra sitting room and guest quarters. Its chief problems were the angled corner walls and sloping ceiling. Steps on either side and banisters gave it an open feeling and also posed problems for grouping furniture successfully. To reduce the feeling of narrowness and make the area appear more squared-up in dimension, end walls were painted deep orange (only one wall is shown). This color helps to pull the walls in for a squarer and cozier look. The side wall and ceiling were painted white for contrast in the corner. An orange-and-blue patterned carpet further reduces the barren look and its large pattern visually widens the floor space. Since there was little wall space it was impossible to use much furniture; the choice was modular seating units that form a semi-U-shape at one end. The blue, black, white and orange fabric on these pieces is cheerful and also distracts the eye so that it is pulled towards the corner. One section of the modular units is a hide-a-bed for accommodating overnight guests. Note how the solid large scale of the modular units counteracts the open feeling created by the banisters. A strong painting and other accessories produce even more eye interest at the seating-sleeping end of the room.

PROBLEM: Old-fashioned bathroom badly cut up by narrow dividing walls that create three unbalanced alcoves.

SOLUTION: Unification through the use of wall covering and the addition of a built-in unit plus shelves.

An old-fashioned bathroom, divided by several small walls that created awkward alcoves, seemed to defy decoration at first glance. But interior designer Alan Long used these oddities to advantage in this handsome revamp. To counteract the broken-up feeling he covered the entire room with a plaid wall covering in white over-patterned with red and blue. Apart from unifying the area, the wall covering helps to camouflage the architectural defects. This is because the plaid design flows uninterruptedly from one area into the next. The designer also used it on the ceiling (not shown here) for complete coordination in the room. The previously wasted alcove next to the washbasin was given a built-in cupboard trimmed with matching wall covering for a custom-made feeling. This provides much needed storage space and a vanity for accessories; two shelves were added above the cupboard and these house bath linens. Apart from maximizing the use of space, the built-ins introduce a furnished appearance to the alcove. The adjoining niche with the washbasin was similarly dressed up with a mirror and shelf for toiletries. The longer alcove at the end of the room, containing the bath, was treated to floor-length red plastic shower curtains. These can be drawn across the entire area for total privacy when required. The plaid pattern helps to produce an open, airy feeling and extra height in the small bathroom and the white vinyl floor underscores this look.

PROBLEM: Sloping eave, jutting out to create an odd angle and cutting into flow of window wall; exposed radiator.

SOLUTION: Unique treatment of area under the eave; removal of radiator; built-ins to utilize space well.

The large sloping eave that jutted out to create a peculiar niche and which awkwardly cut up the window wall was the main architectural defect in this girl's room. The exposed radiator was unsightly and also broke up the wall, making it difficult to decorate. The haphazard arrangement of the furniture and the large bed unevenly broke up the floor space and gave the room a cluttered, messy look.

Interior designer Abbey Darer knew that there was no way to remove the sloping eave, since it was part of the structure of this bedroom in an old cottage in Maine. Her only alternative was to turn it to advantage in some way and make it a decorative and useful element in the room. She had the inspired idea of building a doll's house under the eave, using the sloping portion of the wall as part of the roof and walls of the doll's house. However, before she began she revamped the entire room to give it a fresh new appearance and to make the best use of the available space. The radiator was removed and a new heating unit was installed in another part of the room. The walls were covered with a crisp blue and white vinyl wall covering which adds airy overtones and is ideal for a child's room since it is easy to sponge clean in a jiffy. A stylized floral vinyl in a mélange of deeper blues and greens went down on the floor and this adds colorful good looks as well as practicality. Soft white curtains with matching ruffled valances were a home sewing project that attractively enhance the windows. With the basic shell in place, the designer built the charming doll's house under the eave, using a large storage box as the base. This has drawers at the front and holds doll's house furniture as well as other small toys. A series of cupboards were built in on either side of the window on the adjoining wall and provide space for clothes and similar items. The niche between them was just the right size for the desk, made out of an old sewing machine base and a wooden shelf. To conserve space even more a smaller bed was bought and this was repositioned to free the floor area in front of the built-in cupboards. The old iron bedstead, trunk and wicker furniture were junk shop "finds," spray-painted white to match the sewing machine base. Such things as the quilt, cushions and tablecloth were other home sewing ideas that help to bring great new looks to the revamped room, which was done on a medium budget.

SMALL AND SQUAT   This type of awkwardly shaped room needs treatments that are the reverse of the ones used in a large, barnlike room. Because the dimensions are confined they need to be opened up visually, so that the room functions well. This can be accomplished by the use of light colors, subdued wall and floor coverings and smaller-scaled furniture.

Color   Neutral tones and pastel shades recede and reflect light, as pointed out earlier. They therefore introduce an airy mood in a small room with a low ceiling that gives it a squat shape. The color scheme you select depends on your personal taste, but the ones which work best are built around such colors as white, primrose yellow, pastel green and blue, apricot and the natural tones such as sand, cement and stone. To open up diminutive dimensions to the fullest, I suggest using a monochromatic scheme. This is based on one color repeated throughout in its various gradations, from very light tones to deeper ones. A monochromatic scheme creates a flowing look because it is used on all areas—walls, ceiling, floor, doors and at the window, as well as for upholstery. It actually leads the eye out and beyond rather than stopping it, as a combination of contrasting colors would do. As you can imagine, the small squat room immediately seems larger and higher because of this flow of one color in various gradations throughout. To avoid a bland look, bright or vivid contrasting colors should be used as accents, in such things as accessories, lamps, pillows and wall hangings.

Here is an example. Let's imagine a room washed throughout with pale yellow. The walls should be the lightest tone of yellow, the ceiling the same color or white to throw it upwards. The floor covering can be the same tone or slightly deeper, such as daffodil yellow. The window treatment, whether it is draperies, shades or shutters, should be exactly matched to the walls to promote a feeling of unbroken space. Upholstery fabrics or materials should match either the walls or the floor covering; wood tones can be anything from light bleached wood to walnut, but no darker. If you wish you can use lacquered furniture, in colors such as white or yellow. With this all-yellow monochromatic scheme in place, you then add color interest with cushions, table-top accessories, lamps, paintings and prints. Green, shrimp, coral, purple, rose pink and blue are good accent colors with yellow.

Wall coverings   To my mind that good old standby, paint, is undoubtedly the best product to use on the walls of a small, squat room. However, if you wish to introduce some pattern or texture you can select wood paneling, wallpaper or fabric. If you like the idea of using wood paneling, always choose one that is light in tone, such as birch, bleached oak or pine. Avoid dark woods as they will reduce dimensions considerably. Wall coverings that have a textural look rather than a pattern, such as silk or grasscloth, are ideal because they do not visually diminish space. Stay away from all strong or large-scaled patterns, which tend to advance into the room. Look for patterns that are light, airy and open, such as trellises, basket weaves, stripes and plaids. Colors should always be light in tone. The same guidelines should be used when you are selecting fabrics for the walls; lightly-scaled patterns, self-patterns and textural designs produce the best effects in a small area. Reflective materials can work magic because they help to push walls out and so expand the space enormously. Silver Mylar papers, chrome and copper panels are effective, but of course mirror is undoubtedly the ideal material because of its three-dimensional qualities. One or two walls covered with mirrored panels or tiles will make any area of space seem three or four times as large.

For the best effect always run mirror floor-to-ceiling and be certain that it is reflecting interesting objects, such as a good furniture arrangement, a wall grouping of pictures, or a table or console decorated with handsome accessories.

Floor coverings   Any wall-to-wall floor covering in a solid color will visually stretch space in a little room. This could be carpeting, vinyl, sisal matting, brick or wood but it must be unpatterned and if possible in a fairly light color. Patterned floor coverings tend to reduce the spacious look and dark colors have the same effect. If you are a stuck with a wood floor that seems far too dark for the room, you can have it refinished in a lighter wood tone, or it can be painted white. In this instance, the white floor paint must then be sealed and protected by several coats of clear polyurethane varnish.

An area rug or carpet only works well in a small room if it is large enough to cover the majority of the floor. Small area rugs tend to create a cluttered feeling because they visually break up the clean sweep of the floor space. It is also a good idea to avoid shaggy, fluffy or hairy piles in a tiny room; smooth, sleek textures are the most appropriate; consider wood, vinyl, low-pile carpeting. Stay away from shag carpeting, Flokati rugs, long-haired or fluffy imitation furs and skins.

Furniture   Obviously you have to be most selective about the furniture you use in a small, squat room. It has to be appropriately scaled to fit into the confined dimensions and only necessary pieces should be included. Under no circumstances should you use lots of little pieces, as

63

you will create a cluttered, crowded look; also avoid lots of leggy pieces, as these distract the eye and create a "forest" look at floor level. Several medium-sized pieces usually work the best in a small room, balanced by one or two lightly-scaled or small-scaled items. The most successful way to furnish a small room is to use one important furniture arrangement that works well for the room's basic function. This furniture arrangement can then be balanced by individual pieces of furniture that do not take up too much space, along with handsome lamps, attractive wall groupings of art, accessories and plants. In this way you create a harmonious whole, with any odd corners or blank wall space cleverly filled out for a finished look.

PROBLEM: *Protruding fireplace on an angled wall, two windows of different sizes, exposed radiators.*

SOLUTION: *Ceiling beams, clever window treatments and paint.*

Because of its peculiar shape this living room seemed awkward to plan and decorate. But by working around the fireplace and the oddly angled wall, instead of attempting to disguise them, they were turned into special features of the room. The high and low windows were brought into alignment through the use of clever treatments.

The first step in this revamping was stripping the walls of the lightly patterned paper. They were then painted a spanking white, as was the ceiling, for a fresh, crisp look. White tends to push walls out by visual illusion and so helps to open up an area; use of one color throughout helps to make architectural defects appear less obvious. To pick up the rustic mood of the brick fireplace, the ceiling was given beams. These are actually made of a plastic that simulates the look of old wood and is easy to handle. The beams are simply glued into place with an adhesive. The clever placement of the beams above the fireplace helps to bring it into line. It seems less awkwardly shaped by sheer visual illusion. The beams add a sense of balance and draw the eye away from the angled fireplace wall. The windows were too modern in feeling for the traditional mood being created decoratively, so each one was given a handsome camouflaging treatment. The one nearest the fireplace was disguised with floor-to-ceiling floral draperies and a matching Roman shade. Apart from hiding the ugly window they introduce added importance and lend a more balanced look to the room as a whole. Placement of the antique console table in front of the window is a simple way of concealing the exposed radiator. The other window was given an entirely different treatment and although it is not shown in the "after" photograph it should be mentioned. Shelves were built all

around the window in the manner of a giant frame, and a window seat was built along the wall below. This structural treatment helped to bring the smaller window, set high on the wall, into better proportion with the other larger window. A section of the window seat can be seen in the photograph. It was made of sturdy plywood, painted white and topped with white fabric cushions. Each end was left bare to house plants and accessories and to act as serviceable end tables. The long sofa adds balance on the wall next to the fireplace, as do such accessories as the mirror and antique candelabra. The small area rug links this furniture grouping with the window seat and leads the eye away from the fireplace.

ALCOVE   An alcove generally creates an irregular look because it breaks up the even flow of a wall. However, this is not necessarily a detriment to the room, since it sometimes introduces character. You can go in two different decorative directions in this awkwardly shaped room. You can turn the alcove into a decorative asset by playing it up or you can disguise it through a little clever camouflage.

Highlighting   To bring an alcove into special focus you have to treat it quite differently from the rest of the room. Basically this means giving the walls of the alcove their own special treatment and using furniture and accessories in the alcove to make it a strong center of decorative interest.

For example, if you plan to use a wall covering on the majority of the walls, treat the alcove itself to paint, selecting a shade that coordinates with one of the colors in the wall covering or one which adds interesting contrast. Alternatively, you can line it with mirror, silver Mylar, fabric or a wall covering that is designed to coordinate with the one used in the rest of the room. In this way you will make the alcove stand out so that it becomes an eye-catching focal point. You can then add a striking piece of furniture or handsome accessories to introduce dramatic impact.

Here are some ideas for highlighting an alcove. Use mirror to cover the walls and then place a steel-and-glass etagere on the back wall. Fill this with all manner of accessories plus a few plants and a lamp. This combination is designed to create a sparkling effect, along with interesting double images, and is ideal in a small room. If you cannot afford to use panels of mirror, buy inexpensive mirrored tiles or utilize silver Mylar paper instead. When an etagere is either too large or too costly for your budget, replace it with a steel-and-glass table or a plexiglass table. Add a metal or clear glass lamp and accessories, and then balance the table with a tall plant placed on the floor. Yet another alternative arrangement is to use lots of plants and a floor lamp in the sparkling alcove, and this is especially useful if you cannot afford to buy furniture. I must point out that some sort of lighting is essential in the alcove when you use mirror or any other reflective materials, to create the glittering effect. A striking piece of furniture also shows up to advantage against a mirrored or reflective backdrop. You might consider a porcelain stove; a small, brilliantly lacquered piece of chinoiserie; a small antique chest or console; a piece of handpainted furniture or one decorated with decoupage; or any unusual piece of furniture that is eye-catching.

Another idea is to turn the glittering mirrored alcove into an art corner. Place several pedestals, graduated in size and height, in the alcove and use them to display pieces of sculpture. For added effect, hang a strong painting or a large mirror in a period-style frame on the back wall. Incidentally, all of the pieces of furniture and the ideas just mentioned can be utilized in an alcove that does not have a mirrored or reflective backdrop. But always be sure to include a lamp or lighting to focus attention on the object or objects being shown off.

If you have a collection of unusual or interesting objects, you can suspend a series of glass shelves from the ceiling level to the center of the back wall, and use them to display your collection. Add a small console or Parsons table to complete the wall and to hold a lamp.

Interior designer Jane Victor often turns an alcove into a flower bower, literally an indoor garden that blooms the year round. If she can find a baker's rack of the right size she utilizes this to hold the plants, otherwise she adds a series of shelves which run along the side walls as well as the back wall. These can be of glass, metal or wood, whichever is your personal choice. The shelves are then packed with all manner of plants, in all shapes and sizes for interest. Jane stresses the importance of including flowering plants amongst the plain green ones, for color and a change of pace. She also recommends the use of small spotlights, placed on the floor and trained on the plants, to focus attention on them. When the plants are displayed on shelves, Jane likes to add a whimsical piece of pottery or garden sculpture on the floor. She prefers ceramic animals, of large or medium height. Don't include anything that is too small as it will look lost and is also in danger of being kicked and accidentally broken. And don't forget that most plants require plenty of light, so be sure to place them appropriately.

If space is at a premium and you need the alcove to be more useful, you can make it function as a writing corner or a seating area. Select a small-scaled writing desk and chair that have good lines and arrange them in the alcove, with the desk and chair facing into the room. For a seating area you can use a small love seat, a chaise or a chair and ottoman, plus a floor lamp or a small table and lamp. But in either instance be sure you have included enough wall accessories to make the alcove stand out as a center of visual interest in the room.

Camouflaging Perhaps the easiest way to camouflage an alcove is to treat it as if it does not exist. By this I mean decorating it as just another wall in the room, carrying the same wall covering over the alcove area so that it blends into the overall background. You can do this whether you use wallpaper, paint, wood paneling, fabric, vinyl or any other wall covering for that matter. Once this has been done, you have to seek out a piece of furniture that fits the size of the alcove exactly. If you are using an armoire, an etagere, or any other large, similar piece be sure that it does not protrude beyond the edge of the alcove walls. Essentially, it should be flush with these walls to create an unbroken flow of wall space. On the other hand, if you are utilizing a sofa or love seat, select one which is deeper than the alcove, so it will protrude slightly into the room. This helps to pull the alcove seating arrangement further into the room for a feeling of balance and at the same time diminishes the alcove effect.

A variety of different built-ins can be used to camouflage the alcove, and they are not necessarily expensive. If you are a book lover, turn the whole alcove into a library area. To do this you must run shelves from floor to ceiling, right across the alcove, so that it is covered entirely. Make the shelves the same width as the alcove so that they finish flush with the side walls. Once the shelves have been filled with books, the alcove is completely hidden from view.

Interior designer Joan Blutter often turns an alcove into a storage unit which is highly decorative at the same time. She begins by running shelves across the alcove, from the floor to the ceiling. She always stops short of the edge, to leave enough room to hang doors on the alcove. For the best effect Joan recommends seeking out beautiful old doors which add distinction to the room, or using any other doors which have decorative interest. Sometimes she has plain wooden doors painted with attractive designs, or dressed up with decoupage or floral cut-outs from wallpaper which are then varnished over with clear polyurethane. If you can find someone to do it and can afford the price, this designer suggests covering the doors with trompe l'oeil designs. But whichever way you dress up the doors, they must always be full length, running from floor to ceiling, so that the alcove is entirely hidden.

Other built-ins which help to camouflage an alcove include banquettes for a seating area, a storage unit with shelves above, and a bar composed of a base storage unit plus wall-hung shelves. All of these must be built out to the edge of the side walls, so that you get a feeling of smooth unbroken space on the wall where the alcove is situated.

I myself once camouflaged an alcove with see-through wooden gates which I had hung across the front of the alcove. I then filled the space behind the gates with masses of green plants. Some of these were placed on the floor, others were suspended from the ceiling, while still more were hung on the back wall in special wall containers. The alcove was totally hidden from view and the effect was of gates leading into a garden. Small spotlights were hidden amongst the foliage and when they were turned on at night the area came alive dramatically.

When the space within the alcove was not required for a specific purpose, I have often camouflaged the alcove with handsome screens. I find that floor-to-ceiling screens are the most effective as they hide the alcove completely. I have also camouflaged an alcove with floor-to-ceiling draperies, hung at the edge of the alcove as if it were a window. Of course the draperies must be kept closed at all times. Strip lighting within the alcove can be added, if you want to create the effect of light coming in through the draperies.

TOO MANY DOORS   A plethora of doors in a room does not exactly create an awkward shape. However, they do break up the normal flow of wall space and make it difficult to decorate a room successfully. If all the doors lead to other rooms then you are literally stuck with them. You can't very well block up entry and exit ways. Your only solution in this instance is to camouflage them as well as you can. The simplest way is to treat them exactly as you have treated the walls. In other words, use the same materials on them. If you have painted your walls dark green, then use the same paint on the doors. They will instantly seem to disappear because they blend into the background. When you have used wallpaper or a wall covering on the walls, then carry this same material onto the doors, again so that they will blend into the background unobtrusively. This rule applies to all types of wall covering and includes fabrics, vinyl fabrics, wood paneling and even mirror if this has been used on a wall broken up by a door. To make the door seem less obviously a *door,* you can sometimes remove hardware that seems too prominent and replace it with smaller, less obvious pieces. If this is not possible, paint the knob the same color as the door, or a color that makes the knob blend into the background of the door, if a wall covering has been used.

If some of the doors in a room open onto closets or cupboards, it is a good idea to have new doors made which fit flush with the wall and have a touch-spring method of opening. When these types of doors have been treated to match the wall, they disappear completely, especially since they have no hardware to give them away. When these cupboards or closets are used infrequently, furniture can be placed in front of them to camouflage them even more. They also provide more unbroken wall space against which you can arrange furniture. Closet doors can also be hidden by tall screens and arrangements of tall plants, if continual accessibility is not a problem.

PROBLEM: *Sloping ceiling, awkwardly placed window on side wall which is cut up by a jutting closet that creates a niche.*

SOLUTION: *Use of wallpaper, wall-to-wall carpet and clever placement of furniture.*

This bedroom, on the top floor of an old house converted into apartments, had attic-like proportions and was extremely peculiar in shape. A large cupboard cut up the window wall and jutted out to create a niche. The sloping ceiling on both sides of the room reduced the height of the walls and made the room seem low and cramped.

That good old standby wallpaper was used throughout and because it sweeps over ceiling and walls in an unbroken expanse it pulls the room together. Because of this unifying effect the architectural defects are less obvious to the eye. The dark blue floral paper is patterned with white flowers set in stripes and this vertical movement continuing up the walls and onto the ceiling tends to create a feeling of much-needed height. All the doors and woodwork were painted a matching dark blue so that they are fairly inconspicuous and blend into the walls. White wall-to-wall carpeting lightens the area and so expands the feeling of space because of its unbroken flow. Clever placement of furniture also helps to distract the eye from the attic-like contours of the room. The brass bed, flanked on either side by an antique chest and a skirted table, all bring a feeling of balance to the back wall, as do the matching white-shaded lamps. To make use of the niche under the window and avoid wasting space, a love seat was found that neatly fits into the area. This is covered in blue and white fabric to repeat the color scheme and is shown here dressed up with needlepoint cushions and an afghan. A gros point rug placed at the foot of the bed adds a raft of soft colors and also helps to define the sitting room end of the bedroom.

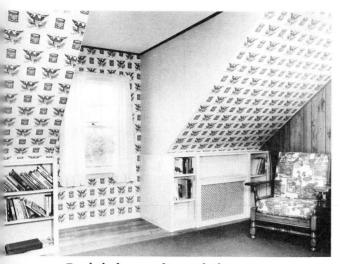

PROBLEM: *Attic room with two sloping eaves on the window wall creating a niche; unattractive bookshelves and a radiator underneath.*

SOLUTION: *Masking of bookshelves with paneling; clever utilization of space under eaves through the addition of built-ins.*

Two sloping eaves were the chief architectural defects in this attic in a Maine cottage. They badly cut into ceiling space and created an unbalanced look at the window end of the room. This was accentuated even more by the use of a large-scale patterned wallpaper on the sloping eaves and in the window area. Bookshelves underneath the eaves were unattractive and also emphasized the uneven proportions of the room. The window alcove proved an awkward space to decorate.

Interior designer Edmund Motyka, who took on the remodeling of this awkwardly shaped attic, was not dismayed by the angled eaves. In fact he saw them as assets that added a certain amount of character and interest and he decided to play them up through clever decorating. He removed the old radiator from the bookshelves on the right, but left the actual bookshelves in place. He attached a sturdy wood shelf, eighteen inches wide, to the top of the right bookshelf, and on this he built three small storage compartments against the sloping wall of the original eave. Once they were completed he ran plywood paneling up from these to the ceiling, following the sloping angle of the eave behind it. The plywood paneling is actually a false eave eighteen inches in front of the original one shown in the "before" photograph. The front of the old bookshelves was masked with the same honey-toned paneling, as were the side walls of the window niche. The designer extended these walls slightly so that they are flush with the edge of the new eave and wider than before. This extra depth enabled Ed Motyka to build in a large, comfortable window seat, fronted with paneling and topped with an upholstered seat. The windows above and on the other wall were treated to louvered shutters made of a similarly light-toned wood; another honey-colored wood was used for the Parsons-style desk which tucks neatly under the right eave. The eave at the left was also built out and extended to match the other for a sense of true balance in the room. Again the bookshelves were fronted with plywood for uniformity and camouflage. The second eave was transformed into a handsome area for the bed, actually a queen-sized mattress anchored into position by a long low footboard that doubles as a table. The four-by-four post running up from the footboard to the ceiling demarcates the area nicely, while its partner running floor-to-ceiling at the other side of the room was included for that needed sense of harmony and balance. Shelves were built on the far wall and filled with corrugated boxes which the designer first spray-painted yellow, orange and green; these file papers and sewing notions. The sewing table, another built-in, also holds similar file boxes in one end. The rest of the attic was treated to paneling while the floor was covered with green cushioned vinyl with the look of handpainted tiles. Tailored bedspread and cushions pick up the

yellow, green and orange tones of the file boxes; they also help to turn the bed into a functional seating unit during the day. The same plaid is used for the upholstery on the window seat. Appearances can be deceiving, as Ed Motyka proves in this attic, by fitting in maximum storage and functions within minimum space through clever use of built-ins that any home remodeler can tackle. The attic gains a whole new look and functions as a home office, a sewing room and a guest room.

WALL JOGS   Unfortunately there is very little you can really do about wall jogs, or those protruding beams that cut into walls to create broken wall space and awkward shapes. The easiest way to camouflage them is to treat them like the walls, in much the same way you would treat doors. In this way they blend into the background and so seem less apparent. Whenever possible, try to hide them with tall pieces of furniture, plant arrangements or screens. When you have a wall broken at each end by a wall jog, you can pull this wall into shape by adding built-in bookshelves between the two protruding beams. If a beam breaks a wall in the center, use the same technique; either build bookshelves along the entire wall so that the beam is lost, or build shelves to one side of the protruding beam. Again the beam will seem to disappear as it becomes part of the bookshelves. Beams which protrude at each end of a window wall can often be camouflaged by the window treatment or draperies used; another way to hide beams on this particular wall is to front them with folding screens painted to match the walls or the window treatment.

Interior designer John Elmo often turns a protruding beam in the center of the wall into an advantage. He uses the beam as a kind of demarcation point in the room. For example, he will place a library table or a Parsons table against the front of the beam, which faces into the room, so that the table juts out into the room. The beam immediately seems less obvious and the beam and the table in conjunction create two distinct areas within the one room. To camouflage the beam even more, this designer will add a tall plant or a small tree in the corner created by the beam and the table. Sometimes John Elmo places an etagere against the front of the beam, with the shelves fronting into the room. Again the beam is hidden because it becomes part of the demarcating etagere.

Obviously, then, it is always a good idea to try and turn these elements that create awkwardly shaped rooms into an advantage, when you cannot camouflage them entirely. As I pointed out earlier in this chapter, awkwardly shaped rooms often have the most character and they can be the most fun to decorate.

PROBLEM: *A staircase flowing directly into the room; wall underneath it cut up by protruding stairs; recessed long wall running length of room.*

SOLUTION: *Wall-to-wall carpet for unifying effect; built-in units on the two awkward walls.*

One of the main drawbacks in this room was the open staircase flowing directly into the room and the awkwardly shaped wall underneath it, which was cut

into by the stairs. Another problem was the long recessed wall which started at the bottom of the stairs and seemed too close to them to decorate effectively. The room, a basement in a suburban home, had previously gone to waste until interior designer Virginia Frankel turned it into a handsome family room through good decorating. Parrot green decorator paneling was used throughout to hide the basement's unattractive concrete walls and the designer also took it up the staircase wall to introduce continuity and make this area a part of the room. She covered both the floor and the stairs with the same wall-to-wall carpet for the same unifying effect. By integrating the stairs in this way they seem less obvious. To fully utilize the awkwardly shaped wall under the stairs, which otherwise would have been unused, the designer built two long shelves that run flush with the protruding steps for visual line-up and balance. A built-in desk below the shelves was tailored to fit neatly into the space and it too adds to the balancing effect created by the shelves. These pieces add a furnished look to this area and help to mask the awkward shape of the wall. Virginia Frankel dimissed the idea of using a furniture arrangement against the recessed wall; instead she had a long unit built to fit the exact size of the recess. This provides storage and functions as a server for snacks, also acting as a spot for the TV and plants. She added a long shelf above for that needed sense of balance; this works as a display surface for books and accessories and holds the stereo speakers. All the built-ins were fronted with parrot green paneling and topped with plastic laminate. This is in a tawny color to pick up the shades in the carpet, and like the paneling it is wipe-clean. The nylon carpet in a mixture of golds and browns is also hardy and ideal for use in a basement. It has its own built-in carpet cushion for extra comfort, sound absorption and insulation and can be installed directly over concrete sub-flooring as it was here. Seating pieces are arranged in the far corner and so free floor space in the center.

75

PROBLEM: *Dining room adjoining a doorless kitchen, plus small slanting corner wall with a window, air conditioner and radiator.*

SOLUTION: *Utilization of window shades, three coordinated wall coverings and wall-to-wall carpeting for integration of both areas.*

This dining room had two basic decorating problems. The dining area flowed directly into the adjoining kitchen which was doorless, and the slanting window wall was out of architectural balance. It was also burdened with an air conditioner and a radiator beneath. Interior designer Peg Walker decided first to integrate both areas through the use of similar green and white wall coverings chosen in three versions of double checks. She used the smallest check on the upper portion of the walls in the dining room, filling in the wall below the dado with a large-scaled and more dominant pattern. This turns the corner into the kitchen to cover two end walls. The main wall of the kitchen, facing into the dining room, was treated to the third wall covering, a design blend of the two patterns featured in the dining area. The use of these pattern- and color-coordinated wall coverings helps to create a feeling of harmony between the two areas; the mélange also distracts the eye from the room's odd shape.

Since she was working on a very limited budget, the designer dismissed the idea of using doors to shut off the kitchen. Instead she came up with an innovative idea that was much less costly. She had a white fiberglass window shade made to fit the wide opening into the kitchen. This was hung at the kitchen side and simply pulls down to act as a room divider and to close off the view of pots and pans during meals. The kitchen light shining through highlights its texture and creates an interesting effect. The designer had a matching smaller shade made for the window in the dining area. This fits neatly within the frame and solves the problem of decorating the awkwardly placed window on the small slanting wall. For example, draperies would have given the window an unbalanced look in relation to the rest of the room and would have interfered with the use of the air conditioner. The shade sits above it during the summer and can be pulled down to hide it when it is not needed. The shade is also budget-minded and by far the cheapest treatment for the window. A narrow shelf was used to camouflage the exposed radiator underneath the window and also provides space for accessories. To complete the feeling of integration between the two areas created by the coordinated wall coverings, the designer ran blue wall-to-wall carpet throughout. Incidentally, the dining area is furnished with moderately priced furniture which you carry home from the store in cartons and put together yourself.

PROBLEM: *Small, oddly shaped entrance hall leading into a raised dining room without doors.*

SOLUTION: *The use of two different types of floor and wall coverings; a play of textures and a two-tone color scheme.*

The main problem in this apartment was the small, oddly shaped entrance hall that opened directly onto a doorless, raised dining room. The owner did not want to go to the expense of putting up doors, which would have also closed up the areas and made both appear cramped. At the same time she wanted to create a feeling of demarcation. Because of the closeness of the two areas it was also important to do this without producing disharmonious decorative looks in the overall space. Interior designer Alan Long was able to achieve the right results by using a two-tone color scheme of black and white for overall integration, plus a play of textures and pattern for design interest. For practical purposes he used gray and slate-colored vinyl tiles in the hall, set down in a random square design. They are hard-wearing and don't show the dirt easily, an important consideration in such a heavy traffic area. Since the hall was small he wanted to expand the feeling of space. For this reason he selected a silver, black and white vinyl, so finely striped it appears to have no pattern at all. The reflective qualities of the wall covering and the vertical effect of the stripes add height and airiness to the area, which immediately seems to be opened up. Also the wall covering's "no pattern" look works well with the more strongly patterned floor covering. In the dining room, the designer reversed the play of patterns and textures to visually demarcate the two areas more effectively. Here the wall covering is a black and white vinyl in a texture-embossed, traditional pattern. This large scale pattern is balanced by a plain gray carpet which does not compete. Although the two wall coverings selected by the designer are entirely different in pattern, they harmonize because the scale of each does not compete with the other and the colors are related. Furniture in the two areas is all lacquered white, except for the eye-catching Chinese Chippendale chairs, lacquered vivid red. They are the only splashes of really bright color in the two areas. Wall coverings are practical, since they are simply sponged clean; carpet is of a man-made fiber and is kept in tip-top shape in the same way. If you want to correct space that is similar architecturally, but cannot afford to put down new floor coverings, simply treat walls in this manner by utilizing two different but related wall coverings.

3 · How to Overcome Space Problems

Almost everyone is suffering from the space squeeze in one way or another today. Some homes are short of rooms, others have rooms that are far too small, while there are those where one room has to function on various levels to cater to a mixture of living needs. One-room studio apartments also present many decorating problems, since this type of room has to work around the clock, efficiently serving living, dining and sleeping needs while looking as attractive as possible at all times.

Ingenuity with furniture and furnishings is the key to successfully decorating rooms so that space problems are effectively overcome. Color works wonders, as do built-in units, double-duty furniture and wall-hung furniture. Well-planned furniture arrangements also help you to make the most of the available space, so that it functions to the best of its ability. Finally, floor and wall coverings that have been carefully selected with an eye to color, texture and pattern contribute a great deal in a room that is short on space.

Any room is easier to decorate when you are working from a master plan and this is especially so when a room has space problems. It is therefore a good idea to make a master plan at the outset and use it through all stages of decorating.

PLANNING

A master plan consists of a floor plan, several alternate furniture arrangements most suitable for the size of the room, some good color schemes and a selection of the most appropriate fabrics, wall and floor coverings.

The best way to begin is to measure the room and make a floor plan. This is quite a simple task and instructions for doing it correctly were given in the preceding chapter. The floor plan enables you to visualize easily the amount of space you have to work with, and it also pinpoints the actual shape of the room and all architectural elements. By carefully studying the floor plan you will be able to decide exactly how much furniture you can include for comfort and good looks, and formulate ideas for the actual furniture arrangements. Always measure the pieces of furniture you are considering using, to be sure they are the right size and to avoid any shocks later. There is nothing worse than finding out that a piece of furniture is far too large for the room, when you have already purchased it.

Lightly pencil furniture arrangements onto the floor plan, erasing until you find the one which is best for the function of the room and its size. With the floor plan and the furniture arrangements completed you can start planning a suitable color scheme.

There are several points you should know about color and the way it works. Always bear these points in mind when you build a color scheme. Pale or light colors recede and so make an area seem larger. They also reflect light and bounce it back into the room, reinforcing the feeling of spaciousness. Dark and vivid colors advance in and so reduce space by visual illusion. Since they absorb light rays they make any room look smaller.

It is logical then to use light or pale colors in a small room or studio apartment, when you wish to promote a feeling of greater size. On the other hand, if you want to underscore the feeling of coziness and intimacy, select deeper or more vivid tones. By utilizing these you can create a jewel-box effect that is both warm and stimulating. A room of generous proportions, which has to function on different levels to combat space problems, can be treated to either light or dark colors, depending on the mood you wish to create and your personal color tastes.

When you are selecting fabrics, wall and floor coverings it is important to pay attention to texture and pattern as well as color. Bear in mind that all very large or dominant patterns advance and generally reduce space to a certain degree. For instance, strong-patterned wall coverings are inclined to pull walls in for a more confined feeling, while pattern on the floor also diminishes the feeling of spaciousness to some extent. Upholstery fabrics with a dominant pattern tend to make furniture look larger than it actually is; similar drapery fabric jumps forward into a room and gives windows more prominence than you might want. For all of these reasons it is usually wiser to select fabrics, wall and floor coverings that are relatively plain, relying on their textural effects for design interest. Certainly textures help to introduce a change of pace visually, without diminishing the feeling of space. Obviously a large room does not always put these restrictions on you; however, remember

PROBLEM: A small, windowless dining area opening off a living room and overlooking a small adjoining entrance hall.

SOLUTION: Use of mirror, wall-to-wall carpet and clean-lined, tailored furniture.

Apart from being small and confined, this dining area in an apartment was also dark and dull. To counteract the lack of windows, add light airiness and sparkle, interior designer Joan Blutter covered the back wall with floor-to-ceiling panels of mirror. This treatment helps to visually expand space, as well as creating extra decorative interest through its reflective quality. It picks up diverse images from the next room and, when the curtains are open there, it mirrors the spectacular view seen from this wall of windows. To open up the dining area further, the interior designer carried the deep blue wall-to-wall carpeting through from the living room. This introduces an uninterrupted flow of color and texture and enlarges the feeling of space. She selected clean-lined, tailored furniture of medium scale, which provides total comfort and function yet does not overly intrude on the very limited floor space. The designer used a neat trick to add extra dimension to the dining area, one which also expands the confined space in the entrance. This was her continuation of the mirror onto the narrow wall at the other side of the floor-to-ceiling divider. As you can see it lightens the entrance and reflects more images. By night the crystal chandelier and candles produce a glittering effect against the mirror.

that lots of patterns can become very boring, even banal after a while, and also tiring to the eye. So make your selections carefully for one-room studios, rooms that function on various levels to suit different living needs, and rooms that are required to live well around the clock.

THE SMALL ROOM

You can make a small room live twice as large, by using your imagination and some clever decorating tricks.

COLOR   This is your most important tool because it can alter the basic size and shape of a room through visual illusion. For example, a color scheme built around light, pale or pastel tones will help to make the tiny room seem twice as large. I like monochromatic color schemes, based on one color used in various degrees of intensity. The smooth flow of one color throughout gives the effect of pushing walls out. It also sends the ceiling soaring and widens the floor space considerably.

Effective monochromatic schemes for small rooms include the following: *Yellow*, starting at pale primrose and gradually deepening to daffodil and jonquil yellows. *Green*, starting with a soft apple or leaf green through gradations of Kelly to emerald. *Sand*, moving from natural stone colorations to deeper mushroom and beige. *Blue*, beginning with soft sky blue and deepening to bluebell and royal blue. *Turquoise*, starting at pale aqua through tones of marine aquas and sea greens. *Peach*, starting at the palest blush tint through to shrimp and coral tones. *Gray*, beginning with smoky hues and moving on to soft lilacs and flannel gray. And of course that good old standby *White on White*, highlighted by fresh flower colors in accents.

If you do not wish to use a monochromatic scheme, some of these other combinations may appeal to you. Yellow, green and white; beige and coral; green and blue; white and blue; white and green; yellow and white; peach and mushroom; aqua and yellow; aqua and lilac; lilac and green; and black and white.

Don't overlook the ceiling when you are planning your color scheme. Remember that all pale colors help to add height, so paint the ceiling stark white or in a slightly lighter tone than the color used on the walls. This latter idea also helps to continue the unbroken feeling of flowing space, because it does not stop the eye but leads it out and beyond.

WALL COVERINGS   If you want to use a wall covering instead of paint, you have the choice of wallpapers, fabrics, vinyl fabrics, wood paneling and mirror. If wallpaper or fabric is your choice, select one that has a light or open pattern; stay away from strong, dominant patterns. If you prefer wood paneling choose light ones, such as birch, pine or bleached oak; avoid all dark wood tones on the walls.

Naturally, mirror is ideal for opening up space in a small room. Used on one or two walls it makes a room seem much larger because it leads the eye out and beyond. It also bounces light back into the room for an airy feeling and its many reflections add decorative interest.

Other reflective materials such as copper and chrome panels and tiles, and silver wallpapers expand the space and introduce airy dimensions. When some of these are used in combination with mirror, striking effects can be created.

Vinyl fabrics that simulate suede and leather are also suitable for small rooms, providing you select light or soft colors which recede. They introduce interesting textural effects on walls, which do much to enhance the room and give it character.

FLOOR COVERINGS   Light colored floor coverings reinforce the spaciousness and today you can happily use white and pastel tones without fear of rapid soiling, discoloration or deterioration. Vinyls are easy to keep pristine and sparkling, as are light-colored or painted wood floors; a polyurethane finish protects them from soiling and scuffing. Even wall-to-wall carpeting can now be practical in white or ice-cream pastels, if you pick one made of synthetic fibers, such as nylon, acrylic, polyester or olefin. All repel staining and soiling and are simple to keep in tip-top condition. For example, I have had white wall-to-wall carpeting in my library-office-guest room for four years and it looks fresh and clean. Made of a nylon fiber, it is simply vacuumed regularly and any spots have been instantly removed by soap-and-water sponging.

If you don't like light or pastel colors on the floor, look at some of the floor coverings in clear, bright tones. It is wiser to stay away from dark colors as they advance and also absorb light, making the floor space seem much smaller.

Naturally, solid-color floor coverings further the spacious look, but you can use patterns if this is your preference. But try to use a pattern that lengthens or widens the room by visual illusion, such as vertical or horizontal stripes, plaids and tartans, or geometrics.

It is worth mentioning here that too many patterns give any room an overly busy look and this is especially so in a tiny room. So keep patterns to the minimum; don't use a patterned floor covering if you have a patterned wall covering, and vice versa.

I do not recommend the use of area rugs in a small room as they tend to break up the even flow of floor space and introduce a cluttered look. However, you can use an area rug or carpet if it covers the entire floor or most of it. Do avoid using lots of very small rugs that create spotty islands of color and texture on the floor. They are not only very distracting to the eye but interfere with the overall feeling of balance.

FURNITURE ARRANGEMENTS   The furniture you select for a small room naturally depends on the actual function of the room. There is always one basic piece which is absolutely necessary to cater to the living needs of the room. In a bedroom or guest room it is the bed which is of primary importance; in a study, a desk or table is the crucial piece; a library requires bookshelves before anything else; and in a dining room obviously the dining table is the most important piece. Always buy this one necessary piece of furniture first, as this is the crux of the room and your furniture arrangement. Everything else is of secondary importance and flows around the anchor piece.

Before discussing furniture arrangements, a word first about the correct scale of furniture to use in a small room. Very large pieces are obviously wrong for a room of minute dimensions, as they create a heavy, somewhat ponderous look and literally take up too much space. At the same time, lots of little pieces don't really work well either, since they tend to produce a busy, cluttered feeling. This is particularly so when you have lots of tiny tables and leggy pieces. The effect is messy and distracting, especially at floor level.

Medium-sized pieces, on a fairly light scale, are generally the best to use in a small room. You can balance these with one or two smaller-scaled pieces and even a tall important item, if it is in a light scale and in a light-toned wood or a see-through material such as glass, plexiglass or plastic; or if it is made of a shiny material like steel, chrome or brass. Incidentally, all of these materials are perfect to use when space is at a premium, since they are airy in appearance and seem to take up relatively little space. It is visual illusion of course, but the effect is ideal in confined dimensions.

When you plan your furniture arrangements for a small room, begin with the basic piece and build around this. If you don't have much space for more than this one basic piece, you can add decorative overtones and a more furnished look with accessories used on the walls. When you have a little more space with which to work, make the basic piece the key in your main furniture arrangement, placing subsidiary items around it. You will probably find you only have the space for one strong furniture arrangement, but you can add the necessary balance with small items, wall accessories and plants.

Undoubtedly the best way to arrange furniture in a small room is to place it against the walls. This frees the central floor area and gives the illusion of more spaciousness. It also ensures easy flow of traffic within the room. This is a major consideration in any room and of vital importance in a small one. People must be able to enter, leave and move around comfortably and without squeezing past furniture in tight groupings that are too close together. So whenever possible, avoid those furniture arrangements which intrude into the center of the room.

WALL-HUNG FURNITURE   One excellent way to gain space is to make the walls work overtime by utilizing wall-hung furniture. By taking advantage of vertical space you will immediately free the floor area and physically and visually expand the dimensions of the room, whatever its size. The wall-hung furniture currently available is well designed and made, and it is styled to work in almost every kind of room. There are pieces appropriate for kitchens, nurseries and children's rooms as well as more general living quarters.

There are all types of wall-hung systems. Some cover only a small section of a wall, others can run full-length along it and even extend onto adjoining walls or turn a corner. Most of the units are designed to be arranged in a variety of combinations to suit many different living needs. They include such components as shelves for books, accessories and hi-fi equipment, storage cabinets, a serving counter or counters, desks and dining tables. The newest imported wall-hung system even includes a bed that flips up and folds away into the unit when not in use. Because of their great flexibility, wall-hung systems provide space to store, arrange, hide or display things as precisely as you wish without infringing on much-needed floor space. You are then left with more than adequate space to include seating and sleeping pieces, and the room itself functions on its most efficient level. Wall systems of furniture are also flexible in that they are designed to work in most rooms and of course they are easy to dismantle and use in another home, should you relocate. Styles are eclectic. You can choose modern or period designs, and materials include a variety of natural wood tones and other finishes.

DUAL-PURPOSE FURNITURE   Another way to conserve space in a small room is to use dual-purpose furniture. This is furniture that serves several purposes while only taking up the space of one piece.

First on the list of course is the sofa bed, sometimes called the hide-a-bed. This looks like a sofa and provides seating facilities; it is available in all sizes and designs. The seat of the sofa opens up, unfolds and pulls out to become a bed, either double, queen or king size, depending on the actual measurements of the piece. Today sofa beds are better constructed and engineered than ever before and provide the ultimate in both seating and sleeping comfort. Styles are designed to blend with any period of furniture, and upholstery materials range from all manner of fabrics to suede, leather and vinyls. One manufacturer now makes a sofa bed in styles identical to regular sofas, so that the two can be used together in a room for a custom-designed look. The sofa bed is perfect to use in a room which needs to have day-time mannerisms and provide seating as well as sleeping facilities—such as a den or study, a guest room, a family room or a teen-age sanctuary.

The Parsons table also serves many needs. It can double as a desk, a dining table, a game or work table and a serving piece. High-low tables also work well in confined space, as they function as low coffee tables and can be flipped up to dining table height. These usually have hinged leaves at the side which open up to extend the surface space for dining. Many modular units provide excellent seating yet can be simply rearranged for sleeping. As these are extremely well engineered and upholstered they are very comfortable. Coffee tables designed as trunks or cubes usually provide storage space inside, a boon when a room is short on built-in cupboards or closets. Then there are attractive small cabinets which make handy end tables, yet also contain a radio or stereo equipment inside. Sideboards and cabinets that contain a television set or stereo equipment can also be utilized for serving in a room short on floor space.

Trundle beds and bunk beds are the perfect solution for small children's rooms, as they conserve space yet offer sleeping facilities for more than one child.

PROBLEM: A medium-sized hall where good space was wasted.

SOLUTION: Utilization of light-scaled furniture, accessories and mirror to create a functional dining room.

This medium-sized hall in an apartment was a total waste of space when furnished simply as an entrance. Since the apartment lacked a dining room, the owners decided to utilize the hallway to the fullest by transforming it into a functional and comfortable dining room. Protruding wall beams that formed a small alcove on one side were covered with easy-to-apply mirrored tiles. The alcove was then lined with a cheerful patterned wallpaper and a strip of the mirrored tiles was carried down the middle of the wall, for extra decorative overtones. A narrow shelf was built across the alcove and this serves as a spot for a lamp and accessories; it also provides support for the back cushions of the banquette. This was made of sturdy wood, covered with a homemade dust ruffle at the front and then topped with comfortable cushions, also homemade. The banquette adequately services the glass-and-chrome table, chosen for its light, airy see-through qualities. Like the chrome-framed chairs and matching stools, it appears to take up little space. For an eye-catching three-dimensional look and expansion of space, the end wall was partially treated to mirrored tiles upon which was hung the handsome white-framed mirror. A matching console with unusual elephant head legs is both decorative and practical since it can be used as a buffet server when required. Attractive lamps and plants help to complete the fresh, summery mood of the entrance hall in its new guise as a dining area. Incidentally, all the furniture is budget priced and was selected because it can be used equally well in other areas of the apartment if necessary.

PROBLEM: *Accommodation of two comfortable seating arrangements plus a piano in a small living room; need to create demarcation between two areas and visually lighten and expand small dimensions.*

SOLUTION: *Use of a raised platform and an area rug for demarcation; visual expansion through utilization of mirrored walls, mirrored screens, small-scale furniture, light wood and shiny materials.*

Interior designer Jane Victor made this small living room in an apartment grow in size and function through clever decorating. The owners wanted to include the piano which had fitted perfectly in their former large living room but which seemed a bulky item for the smaller dimensions here. Because they entertain a lot they required plenty of seating, enough to accommodate eight to ten people at a time. The designer began by building a raised platform at one end of the room. This not only serves to demarcate the room into two distinct areas but creates a feeling of added depth and space because of the change in floor levels. She also made the room seem much larger than it really is through the utilization of mirrored panels on two walls which face each other. The mirror appears to push the walls out and because of its reflective quality it expands the dimensions, also introducing extra airiness as it bounces light back into the room. A protruding beam, the area around windows and a side wall were also lined with mirror, and in combination with mirrored screens in front of the window help to heighten the look of airiness. Another clever trick was the use of white wall-to-wall carpeting on the platform. The uninterrupted flow of the carpet and its pale tones further the illusion of spaciousness. Light-scaled chairs, occasional tables and the sofa were chosen because they fit comfortably into the area and allow enough space for the piano, positioned on a slant at the edge of the platform. The cream brocade and the silver frames of the French chairs carry through the light tones of the carpet and look less bulky; the chunky sofa appears longer than it is through the use of horizontal-striped black and white fabric. In the other area of the living room, the major seating-conversation grouping is pulled together by the handsome area rug. It also defines the grouping and gives it a self-contained feeling. Again mirrored panels running along the back wall create depth and that much-needed look of spaciousness. This wall reflects the raised area. The designer selected light-scaled furniture, mostly tailored in line, to make the most of limited space. She also paid great attention to furniture materials, choosing light woods, polished steel, glass and plexiglass, onyx and marble, as these seem to take up less space by visual illusion. The eye-catching wall covered with hand-painted ancient Egyptian motifs is actually composed of three metal panels which slide across to hide the windows. Panel track lights focus attention on the panels, which easily open when additional daylight is required. The designer created a sleek, unbroken look on both window walls by using these structural-type treatments and so helped to expand spaciousness. In small areas such as these she avoids using individual window treatments, because these tend to break up the flow of a wall and introduce a cluttered, often busy effect.

PROBLEM: Need for both dining and office facilities in a small apartment extremely short on space.

SOLUTION: Utilization of dual-purpose, wall-hung furniture and an area-defining rug in an awkwardly shaped, miniscule foyer.

Space can often be made to work overtime to function on various levels for different and specific activities, through a little clever decorating. Interior designer Peg Walker illustrates just how this is done in this foyer of a small apartment, which was previously unused because of its smallness, awkward shape, and the pass-through into the kitchen which broke up one wall. Peg worked on the premise that what can't go out on the floor can often go up to the ceiling, and furniture that climbs the walls was her answer to the space problems here. She transformed the area into a double-duty corner for dining and paper work, and at the same time added an attractive furnished look to the formerly drab, dull area. The designer selected wall furniture that gave the owner two useful wall storage units, each one only thirty-one inches wide, ideal for these narrow walls. One with bookshelves and base storage cabinet was positioned just inside the front door; the other, also with shelves plus a dining table, was placed on the very narrow wall leading into the living room. The table has a drop leaf that easily accommodates more people when necessary and is serviced by two red plastic chairs, like the wall furniture, of Danish design. An area rug helps to define the dining corner, and its red and blue coloration picks up the tones used in the apartment. Clever arrangement of accessories helps to introduce a highly decorative look; plants, ornaments and paintings interspersed among the books add color and movement.

Here you can see the dining corner transformed into a home office. The wall hung cabinet on the far wall houses a filing system at one side; the other side provides necessary space for the typewriter, stationery and other office utensils which need to be hidden from view at various times. The dining table easily doubles as a desk. This wall-hung furniture, in rich walnut tones, is in the medium price range; shelves and cabinets can be arranged to suit personal preferences and all the pieces are easy to dismantle for relocation to another room or another home.

PROBLEM: *Overly small dining area in an L-shaped living room.*

SOLUTION: *Use of wall-hung furniture cleverly handled in two areas of the room.*

Furnishing the walls when the floor area is extremely limited and confined is a practical way to find additional space. It is also highly attractive since it introduces structural overtones and interesting new dimensions. This is particularly desirable in a room which lacks any interesting architectural overtones, such as this modern apartment living room. Here Edmund Motyka used wall-hung furniture to take advantage of an L-shaped room and to skillfully separate the living and dining areas at the same time. Suspended shelves and cabinets perform different display and storage functions in each area, while flowing around the corner for a pleasing continuity. Shelves and sliding-door cabinets in the living room area provide space for books, hi-fi components, accessories and a lamp, plus records hidden from view in the cabinets themselves. In the dining area they are used for china, silver and linens. In this part of the room the cabinets were strategically hung to leave space for the dining table, which fits neatly between the lower cabinets. Chairs push under the table when not in use, to keep the floor area free. Also, by leaving the floor clear beneath the cabinets, the Danish-designed system helps to maintain the illusion of space in this small apartment. Note how the area rug helps to define the living room and adds to the visual demarcation of the two areas.

PROBLEM: *A small one-room studio with a low ceiling, which had to live well around the clock.*

SOLUTION: *Use of a sofa bed and a matching sofa, plus a large storage display unit; a white and pale-coffee color scheme.*

The owner of this small one-room studio wanted to give it a handsome appearance for living and entertaining, yet it had to function as a bedroom as well. Since the room was relatively small, he decided to expand the space as much as possible by visual illusion and so used a light color scheme to this end. To avoid the overly feminine look produced by too many very light colors, he selected a soft coffee tone for the walls, balancing this with a white sisal floor covering which appears to stretch space underfoot. A white ceiling and the large white units against one wall show up well against the coffee walls and add a feeling of additional height in the room. A matched pair of sofas in sand tones were the ideal solution for both seating and sleeping. One of them is a regular sofa, the other a hide-a-bed sofa that opens up for sleeping. They are identical in style and upholstery, distinguished by upholstered legs and loose cushions against a tuxedo back. The sand-colored fabric is over-patterned with fine black and white stripes for a light plaid look. The floor covering of sisal adds its own tone and texture while sleekly contrasting with the wall units. It is also an inexpensive product for the floor. The wall units are composed of shelves, cabinets and drawers and provide storage and display space for accessories. The two white coffee tables satisfactorily service the two sofas, are lightweight and easy to move around. By restricting his choices to several large pieces, tailored in line, the designer created a spacious, uncluttered look. A large colorful painting adds interest on one wall.

OPPOSITE

PROBLEM: *Small, open-plan living-dining room that needed to be demarcated without creating a cramped look or loss of light in either area; need to visually expand space.*

SOLUTION: *Use of beams and window shades, two different floor coverings and a white and green color scheme.*

This open-plan living-dining room is much smaller than it looks, actually only 24' x 18' in overall dimensions. Designer Edmund Motyka gave it an air of expansiveness through his inventive manipulations of space and clever use of cool, fresh colors. These mixtures of greens and whites do much to introduce light, airy overtones while expanding the feeling of space. The main problem was how to demarcate the two areas for living and dining, without creating a cramped look in either or blocking out light. The designer's clever solution is not only simple to construct but relatively inexpensive and it can easily be copied by any handy person or carpenter. To begin with, the designer positioned two floor-to-ceiling beams in the center of the wide entranceway into the dining room. This immediately introduced a feeling of separateness, which was completed by the addition of three crisp white textured window shades hung between the beams. In combination they act as an unusual room divider when closed, and because they filter light they do not diminish the airy look in either part or produce a cramped feeling. For total coordination within the open-plan room, matching window shades were used at the long window in the living area and at the smaller one in the dining part. The walls throughout were painted white because it reflects light and bounces it back into the room, so making the whole seem much larger. For the same reason white vinyl was used on the floor, but to further underscore the feeling of demarcation created by the beams, the designer used an area rug in the living room. This cleverly defines the seating arrangement here and its mélange of greens, ranging from lime to bottle, repeat the tones used in both areas. The designer selected low seating pieces and coffee tables because the room was lacking in height, balancing these with a tall steel-and-plexiglass etagere in front of one of the windows. This, however, remains relatively unobtrusive because of its see-through qualities. The optical illusion of space is continued in the 9′ x 12′ dining room, where a table, actually a desk pressed into a dining role, stands on crossed chrome legs to mate with steel-framed chairs. These are upholstered in fresh, leafy green and white. This type of room divider can be adapted for other rooms, such as a one-room studio or a room shared by two children.

THE ONE-ROOM STUDIO

A one-room studio apartment needs careful decorating if it is to function successfully, since it has to provide comfortable living facilities around the clock and must look as attractive as possible at all times.

For all of these reasons it is important to have a good decorating plan, one which will guide you through all stages of furnishing and accessorizing. All furniture must be selected with an eye to function, comfort, scale and design. Attention must be paid to color schemes, fabrics, wall and floor coverings, so that you are sure they harmonize well for a smooth whole. Accessories should be chosen to add color and visual excitement.

Begin by making a floor plan of the room, so that you can easily visualize the available space and allocate it accordingly. Select appropriate areas for a seating arrangement, sleeping facilities and a dining spot. Always create furniture arrangements that are workable, both on their own and with each other. Position your furniture so that it functions well where it is and does not have to be constantly rearranged to service specific living needs. There is nothing worse than hauling furniture around when you want to go to bed or have to serve a meal or entertain guests. And remember, a furniture arrangement must look attractive at all times, especially in a one-room apartment where everything is continually on view. As you plan your various furniture arrangements, make allowance for traffic lanes so that it is easy to move around.

COLOR   This is an important element in the one-room studio, perhaps more than in any other kind of home. After all, each one of your living activities takes place in the one room, so its color scheme must please you at all times and on a continual basis. You cannot go into another room and close the door on a color scheme that disturbs you, so be sure you select one you know you can live with around the clock.

It's a good idea to stay away from dark color schemes, for apart from diminishing the dimensions and reducing light, they soon become depressing to most people. Avoid vivid or harsh colors as well, since these jar the eye and are hard to live with over a period of time. Instead look at the softer, blander and more neutral colors. These shades all expand the feeling of space and reflect light, and they are gentle on the nerves. They live well by day, and at night, and they can easily be enlivened with vivid tones used in accents and accessories. Neutrals and light shades make a good background for furniture wood tones, other finishes, and a mixture of fabrics and floor coverings.

WALL COVERINGS   If you do not want to use paint on the walls of your studio apartment, you can choose from wallpapers, fabrics, vinyl fabrics and wood paneling. If your taste runs to paneling, select a light wood tone as this is much easier to live with over a long stretch. Dark woods visually pull in the walls and can create an overpowering or confined feeling.

Should you decide to use a wallpaper or fabric, pay close attention to the pattern. It is wise to avoid large-scaled, strong and dominant patterns, since these can quickly become tiring, even boring to live with after a while. Walls cover the greatest amount of unbroken space in a room and are continually on view. For this reason it is best to use airy, open and light-scaled patterns as, like plain paint, these are restful.

FLOOR COVERINGS   It is better to select a floor covering that is hard wearing and easy to maintain, rather than one which will quickly show signs of wear and dirt. Obviously a studio apartment takes a great deal of abuse because you are living in it around the clock, so be sure the floor covering can withstand this heavy traffic. Also, when living takes place in one area of space, accidents with food and drink are bound to happen. Choose a product that is simple to clean.

Vinyl tiles are ideal, as are all the carpets of man-made fibers such as nylon, polyester, acrylic and olefin. They spot-clean with soap-and-water sponging and many of them have built-in soil-repelling qualities. Wood floors hold up well and they can be stained a dark tone and polished, or coated with a light-colored paint. Whichever method you use on a wood floor, it's a practical idea to give the floor a few coats of clear polyurethane. Apart from adding a sheen and sealing the finish, polyurethane protects the wood from scuffing.

Wall-to-wall carpeting is especially recommended for a one-room studio, since this introduces comfort, absorbs noise and produces a feeling of extra spaciousness, plus a smooth, flowing look. It also links furniture arrangements to each other most effectively. Area rugs tend to break up the space; however, they can be utilized when you want to define specific areas within the room or pull a furniture arrangement together. Whichever type of floor covering you use, always pay careful attention to the color and pattern. Remember, dark colors and large patterns usually tend to reduce the size of a room; pattern can also create a busy effect.

FURNITURE   The basic furniture requirements in a one-room apartment are seating units, a bed, dining furniture and good storage pieces. Obviously the bed must be disguised, if you want the room to live well during the day and not look like a bedroom. You have several alternatives. If you live alone you can use a single bed fitted with a tailored spread, upholstered bolsters and pillows, so that it works as a seating unit by day; you can utilize a daybed which usually comes with top and bottom frames and looks like a sofa; or you can select a sofa bed, which is a sofa and a bed combined. I consider the latter the wisest investment as it has the best appearance and is comfortable. It can also be used in a den or guest room should you move to a larger home.

Incidentally, in a one-room apartment shared by two people, the sofa bed is the most realistic to use. It opens up to double, queen or king size, depending on the one you have purchased.

Several comfortable chairs will supply the extra seating required, and if you have the space available you can add an ottoman or two comfortable stools to make a sizeable arrangement. If possible, use these seating pieces in conjunction with your sofa bed, for a well-rounded conversation grouping.

If space permits, you can select a regular dining table, preferably one light in feeling. A glass-topped table is ideal because it seems to take up little space; light wood tones or light-colored lacquered tables also work well. Stools or chairs can be used, whichever are the most practical in the available space. But also pick those that are light in scale. When you have to conserve space to the fullest, purchase a dual-purpose dining table—either a Parsons table that can function as a desk as well, or a circular unfinished wood table with a floor-length cloth. This can be used to hold a lamp and accessories when not required for dining. The high-low coffee table that rises to dining height is also an excellent piece to use in a studio room.

The wall-hung furniture systems mentioned earlier in this chapter are particularly suited to one-room apartments. By taking advantage of vertical space on the walls, you free the floor area for seating pieces and other items. Wall-hung systems usually come with excellent storage facilities. If wall-hung furniture is not to your taste or if you cannot afford it, look at regular storage units, such as chests and armoires. Choose those pieces which are best suited in scale to the size of the room.

Decorative items that add a finishing touch to a room are of great importance in a one-room apartment, for the color and life and visual interest they introduce. Paintings, prints, posters, mirrors and tapestries can all be grouped on a wall to create a center of eye interest. Plants create living color and help to bring the outdoors inside for a garden feeling. Lamps, table-top accessories, sculpture and books are other items that give a room a personal touch and also reflect your tastes.

PROBLEM: *A small basement required to function as a family-guest room; need for lots of seating and storage plus a bed.*

SOLUTION: *Built-in platform and end tables which double as storage units; the addition of a double foam rubber mattress and masses of cushions.*

When interior designer Abbey Darer was asked to convert a basement into a family-guest room her main problem was overcoming lack of floor space. The owners had several requirements. They wanted plenty of seating and storage space, plus sleeping facilities for the occasional guest, and they wanted to decorate on a limited budget. To save money as well as space, the designer dispensed with regular furniture and instead designed an L-shaped platform along one wall to function for seating as well as sleeping. This platform also contains storage compartments in each end. The sturdy wood platform was covered with plywood paneling, which was also carried up onto the walls to give the basement a "furnished" look. She then had four small tables made, each covered in matching paneling. The two tallest tables were placed at one corner of the platform and act as serviceable end tables. The two smaller tables can be positioned anywhere in the room for convenience; they are here shown together in the center of the L-shape. All four tables have hinged tops which lift up to reveal roomy storage space for bed linens, records, magazines and other items. The designer added a comfortable foam rubber mattress, double in thickness, on the largest part of the platform. This is covered in stretch jersey wool. It provides comfortable seating, yet easily makes up into a bed when required. A collection of pillows in vivid Jack Lenor Larsen fabrics provides rafts of color on the platform, while larger ones show up on the floor. A TV-stereo entertainment area was arranged along the other two walls, not shown in photograph.

PROBLEM: Large, barn-like living room with old-fashioned architectural elements, opening onto two other medium-sized rooms without dividing walls or doors; poor window.

SOLUTION: Use of warm, related colors to counteract barn-like feeling, plus clever mixture of materials and skillful furniture arrangements to introduce definition of each area without destroying flowing feeling between them.

Although the owners of this apartment liked its spaciousness, at the same time they were dismayed by the cold, barnlike dimensions and the general old-fashioned appearance. They were also aware that the small window was out of scale for the overall proportions of the room. Other disturbing elements of the window wall were the exposed radiator and the protruding beams at each end which cut into the flow of this wall, creating an uneven look. Beams running along each side wall, well below ceiling level, were also awkward architectural items which cut into these walls. Finally, for the size of the room, the ceiling was rather low.

Yet another problem was the basic floor plan of the general living areas. The living room itself opened into another area, the only demarcation being a rise in the floor level up two steps and two curved, iron side railings. This area, opening directly off the living room, in turn opened onto another space adjoining the kitchen, again without benefit of dividing doors. To add two sets of louvered doors in the arched entrances would have not only been costly, but, just as importantly, they would have cut off the windowless central area from the only natural daylight, in the living room. The smaller section of space beyond this, next to the kitchen, did have a small window, but was inadequate to serve the central area well. As you can see, ceiling beams, protruding side beams and dados in these two areas only served to create an uneven look.

The owners were confronted with the difficult problem of furnishing a huge expanse of space successfully, a task just as problematical as decorating a small space. They had three basic requirements: they wanted to counteract the cold, barnlike look of the living room; they needed to clearly define each area of the entire floor space, yet without breaking up the spacious flow between the three areas; they needed to introduce lots of light into the central area which was windowless. Their living needs were equally clear and precise: a comfortable living room geared to entertaining; a library-study; a dining room. They also required the apartment to be easy to run, maintain and care for. Interior designer Ving Smith was brought in to help conquer and solve all the problems inherent in these adjoining living areas, which as a whole created something like a "railway car" look, of much larger proportions of course. The designer began by creating an interesting color scheme mainly based on dark blue, deep red, white, rust and natural sand and stone tones; the scheme, in three different variations, was to run throughout the three rooms for coordination and real visual harmony. He also selected a variety of materials with diverse textures, plus light and dark woods, copper, glass and brass, which all contributed a subtle change of pace in each section. The designer began in the living room, shown here. He painted the ceiling white, carrying the white down over the molding that stops at the edge of the wall beams. The white paint adds much needed airiness and a feeling of height; it also helps disguise all the odd architectural elements at ceiling level, since they blend up into the ceiling itself. His next step was to paint the walls dark blue. The blue, carried up over the side wall beams, helps to make them less apparent. However, although dark shades tend to camouflage a multitude of architectural sins, they also absorb light. For this reason the designer used a lacquer paint, because its glossy, glass-like finish bounces light back into the room. The floor was stained a dark mahogany, as in fact were all the floors in this triple living area. With the basic shell in place, the next problem Ving Smith tackled was the old fashioned window, plus the window wall badly cut up by the end beams and the exposed radiator. The designer disguised all of these elements in one fell swoop, and at the same time gave the window added importance by creating a treatment that covered almost the entire length of the wall. Floor-to-ceiling translucent curtains went up first and were then topped by three tie-back draperies and a unifying valance. The draperies at each end skillfully conceal the side beams, while the valance hides the beam at ceiling level. The vertical striped fabric was specifically chosen because it helps to suggest extra height, as do the old doors used as screens to balance the draperies. Pulling together the rest of the room was relatively easy. The dark blue area rug, cut from broadloom carpeting, reiterates the wall color and anchors the major seating arrangement. This is composed of two sofas which face each other across a coffee table; an antique eighteenth-century French hutch flanked on either side by paintings and prints, which becomes the strong focal point in the room; clever placement of the art work, which adds to the feeling of height created by the hutch and balances this piece well. The major seating arrangement is completed by a Parsons table and chair placed behind one of the sofas. The sofas have polished brass frames and the upholstery is white vinyl, chosen for its leather-like appearance and easy-care properties. A similar vinyl that simulates suede was used on the Victorian chaise, to give this an updated look; an old Victorian stand was topped with white plastic laminate and this makes a roomy surface for lamp and accessories, also adding a light look against the blue wall. The window wall is enlivened with plants and a table skirted with the same fabric as that of the draperies, for a coordinated feeling. Finally, the designer put a panel track of lights on the ceiling, immediately over the seating arrangement, for plenty of illumination in this area; table lamps provide pools of extra light in specific areas of the room (*see photo next page,* another view on page 170).

OPPOSITE TOP

Here you can see the area which opens immediately off the living room and which Ving Smith decorated as a handsome and comfortable library. He began by lining the walls with a sand-colored vinyl which simulates suede and creates a change of color pace, yet harmonizes well with the living room behind it. He then built an arrangement of bookshelves on the main wall, facing these with mirrored copper for a light look. Diffused lighting was contained in the top portion of the shelves at ceiling level and the shelves were skillfully arranged to leave a spot for the sofa bed. The wood frame and sand-rust tones of the upholstery blend well with the wall, as does the tub chair covered in the same vinyl used on the walls. Mirrored copper cubes service the seating arrangement and because of their reflective surface appear to take up little space. A collection of South American stirrups makes an unusual decorative statement above the sofa bed; a deep red area rug adds a touch of bright color on the dark wood floor. The small awkward space is utilized to the fullest, since it can accommodate an overnight guest when necessary. The white ceiling and panel of diffused lighting help to add height to the room, while sand tones and copper finishes create a feeling of spaciousness.

The third area of space adjoining the kitchen was transformed into a comfortable dining room full of rich, warm color. The walls were painted red, in a slightly lighter tone than the carpet. Dados were picked out with white paint to match the louvered doors opening into the kitchen. For coordination with the living room, the small window was given the same tie-back draperies made of striped cream and rust fabric. Since this last area was relatively small, Ving Smith selected a glass-topped dining table framed in brass, which is light and airy looking. He partnered this with antique oak dining chairs with high cane backs and cane seats. The seat pads are of deep blue vinyl which matches the color of the living room walls. An old Victorian washstand with a white marble top and backsplash fits neatly into the corner near the window and houses accessories; a sideboard (not shown in photograph) placed on the opposite wall provides serving facilities. The crystal and metal chandelier supplies plenty of illumination over the table.

PROBLEM: *Tiny foyer, dark and dull, cut up by doors, with no real wall space for placement of furniture.*

SOLUTION: *Mirrored panels used on the wall under stairs; addition of a lucite table, area rug and accessories.*

Many foyers are difficult to decorate because of their small dimensions and this one was no exception. Interior designers Bernice Marcus and Anita Rapfogel took on the renovation and redecoration and their aim was to expand the feeling of space and introduce a welcoming atmosphere. They used mirrored panels on the walls under the stairs and this immediately opened up the area, giving it much-needed height, width and depth, as well as sparkle. To further the illusion of light airiness they selected a lucite console table for the stairwell area. The designers preferred this material to wood, which they felt was too heavy in appearance for this tiny wall space. Since there was no other wall space to place furniture against they decided to play up the floor. They selected a 4' x 6' area rug that picks up the wine, red and blue tones of the stair carpet; its contemporary sculptured design produces a dramatic color-pattern point. The actual design of the rug pulls the eye towards the mirror and the beautiful French clock on the wall. Small accessories were used to add finishing touches to the foyer, which looks twice as large after its clever revamp.

PROBLEM: *A small room that had to function as an office for two people; need for three work surfaces plus lots of storage.*

SOLUTION: *Two desks angled to form an L-shape with a divider panel for privacy; a drawing board plus floor-to-ceiling built-in cupboards and bookshelves.*

Interior designer Virginia Frankel required a functional office in her apartment. The main problem was the size of the room, which seemed at first too small to accommodate herself and her secretary. But through clever manipulation of space and some well-thought-out furniture arrangements she created a compact and efficient office extremely comfortable for two to share. She positioned a narrow yet adequate desk in the center of the room which immediately divided the room into two halves. She then placed her own desk up against one end of the narrower desk to form an L-shape, adding a small dividing panel about twelve inches high between the two. This baffles the sound of the typewriter and also creates a degree of privacy without cutting off the light from the window. Behind her own desk, below left, she ran a series of cabinets from floor to ceiling which provide storage for all office supplies. These cabinets continue along an adjoining wall. An open-fronted bookshelf fitted neatly on top of the narrower desk, close to the wall, while another large one was built next to the window. These two bookshelves help to create an alcove for the drawing board. Once these major pieces of furniture were in position, the designer lined the ceiling, small wall areas and the sides of the bookshelves with a green and white lattice paper. This, plus all the white work surfaces, doors and window shutters, helps to open up the small room considerably. Desks and drawing board were all finished with a white plastic laminate for durability and ease of maintenance; pink polyester carpet was chosen for its wearability and easy-care properties; bi-fold doors are a ready-made product that comes in various sizes. Placement of the hanging light fixture in between the desks illuminates both, and telephones are handy for both occupants of the office.

Below right, the office from another angle, showing a close-up of the secretary's desk. This is actually a long table made to accommodate a filing cabinet underneath. The typing chair was slipcovered in the same floral fabric used on the wicker chairs, for continuity. The steel bi-fold doors hide everything when closed and, painted white, they visually expand the feeling of space in the room.

PROBLEM: A one-room apartment required to function for living, dining, entertaining and sleeping.

SOLUTION: Utilization of a space-expanding color scheme; light-scaled furniture and a handsome sleep sofa.

Apart from the fact that this one-room apartment had to function on a variety of levels for many living needs, it had several defects. These were the unattractive window wall and built-in radiator unit; a low ceiling and architectural elements that were somewhat old-fashioned. However it did have certain assets, such as a fireplace, a good wood floor and two distinct areas that could be decorated to function for specific activities.

First step in the revamping of this one-room apartment was the removal of the protruding work surface attached to the built-in radiator unit. The old-fashioned bookcase was also torn out. The whole room was then painted spanking white to introduce a light, airy look. The floor was refinished in a light teak color for the same reason. The long radiator unit was lacquered white so that it blends into the background. To give the window wall a unified look, protruding end beams and wall space between windows were covered with a green and white wall covering. A matching fabric was laminated onto window shades and used to cover the valance that runs the length of the window wall. This clever treatment is not only inexpensive to do, but it adds handsome overtones and disguises poor architectural elements. To further enhance this area, the built-in unit was turned into an indoor garden through a collection of small plants. The formerly wasted space in the window area was now ready to be decorated as a dining corner. This was easily done with the addition of a steel-and-glass dining table, which can also double as a desk when needed. Along with the cane-and-steel chairs the table helps to further camouflage the built-in radiators. A tall steel-and-glass etagere was the perfect piece to round out this area, and it fits snugly into the niche on the short end wall. It is a useful storage-display unit and adds balance here. The major seating pieces and the sleep sofa were grouped in front of the fireplace. This wall was given new decorative dimensions through the use of a mirror, the frame covered in matching wall covering to relate it to the window wall.

The hide-a-bed sofa was placed against the wall facing the fireplace. Because of its light cream upholstery and tailored lines it appears to take up little space. An inexpensive straw area rug was used to define the sleeping-seating area. Two yellow tub chairs, also light in scale, provide additional seating by day and are easy to move when sofa bed is opened up. Lightweight plastic cubes were chosen for the same reason, and because their see-through quality helps to expand space. The sofa bed is flanked by a light-looking glass table and one skirted in the same green and white fabric used for the window wall. Both tables plus their attractive lamps provide adequate service during the day as well as at night, when the area becomes a bedroom. The tall, ceiling-high screen hides an assortment of wicker baskets used to store table, bath and bed linens. The cool, spacious look produced by the play of green and white is enlivened by the yellow chairs, orange and yellow cushions and the floral painting. The finished result is a handsome one-room apartment that lives well around the clock yet does not reveal its nighttime function.

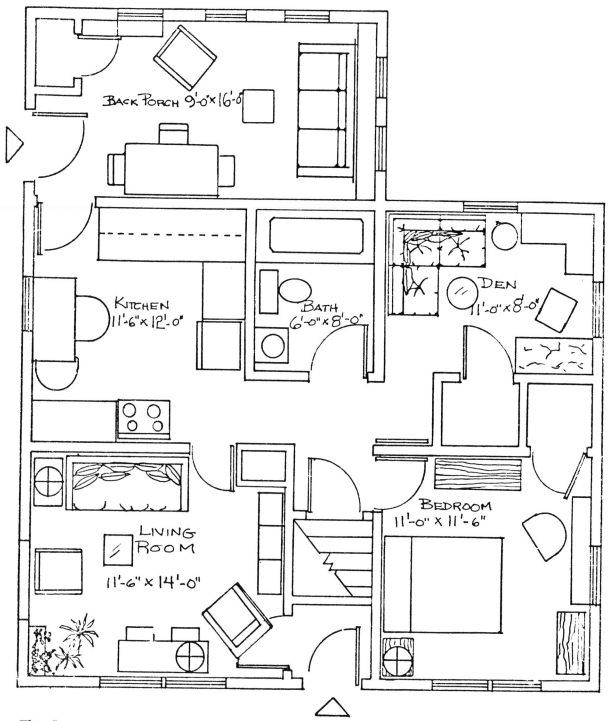

BACK PORCH 9'-0" x 16'-0"

KITCHEN 11'-6" x 12'-0"

BATH 6'-0" x 8'-0"

DEN 11'-0" x 8'-0"

BEDROOM 11'-0" x 11'-6"

LIVING ROOM 11'-6" x 14'-0"

This floor plan shows the basic layout of the house and gives the exact sizes and placement of all the rooms.

PROBLEM: *A small house, with very small rooms, several opening onto each other; lots of windows breaking up wall space; exposed radiators.*

SOLUTION: *One neutral, space-expanding color scheme used throughout; lots of diverse textures for a change of pace; sleekly tailored furniture for an airy, uncluttered look.*

This small house had equally small rooms that needed careful decoration to give them a feeling of spaciousness and make them function comfortably.

This is just one area of the 11′ x 14′ living room, showing door awkwardly placed in corner and window which cuts into wall space.

Interior designer Elroy Edson took on the total redecoration of the house. To produce a harmonious, flowing feeling between all the small rooms and introduce a feeling of spaciousness he used one light neutral color scheme throughout. Pale sand tones cover most of the floors and walls in the rooms, highlighted by deeper, brighter colors used as accents. He created excitement and interest through the contrast of textures rather than by bold colors. To further expand the feeling of space he selected tailored, modern furniture that creates an airy, uncluttered look in the tiny rooms. The designer covered all the walls and the ceiling with a soft sand-colored wall covering in a cork-like pattern which introduces a textured look. He used cream wall-to-wall carpet on the floor, which stretches space underfoot. Although the carpet is very light in color it wears well since it is made of man-made olefin fibers that hide soiling and can easily be spot cleaned. Since the glass door, actually the front entranceway to the house, was never used it was curtained off to add more wall space to the room. Draperies for both this and the window are of cream, lightly overpatterned with tan stripes. Elroy Edson placed all the furniture around the room against the walls, leaving an open area in the center. This furniture arrangement produces an airy atmosphere. The rust velvet sofa, cane-and-chrome chair and brown leather armchair provide adequate seating; the upholstered benches under the upholstered Parsons table can be pulled out when additional seating is needed. The dark brown storage-display unit suggests extra height and fits neatly into the corner near the curtained door, an area that could have been wasted space.

This long narrow room is actually the enclosed sun porch which also acts as an entrance to the house. Designer Elroy Edson decided it was wasted space as it was, and turned it into an attractive dining room that also serves as a guest room for the occasional overnight visitor.

A long, narrow room is always intrinsically hard to decorate. Invariably it needs to be given a squared-off look whenever possible, usually through visual illusion. Elroy Edson did this with a little skillful decorating, clever placement of furniture and the color scheme he selected. Since pale colors tend to recede, he used light sand on the walls to push them out, balancing the light tone with dark brown on the floor, because this advances and so pulls the floor space in for a less elongated appearance. He also thought a dark-colored carpet would be more practical for this heavy traffic area and chose one of olefin fiber that resists dirt and staining. The unattractive double windows were treated as one long one and the draperies immediately added a more balanced look to the end wall. To pull this wall further into the room, the designer grouped furniture and accessories under the window. A comfortable sofa, which opens up into a bed for guests, is backed up against a sofa table holding a lamp, plant and accessories. These introduce color and movement and the whole arrangement advances into the room most effectively. Yet another effective grouping for this narrow room is the dining set. This is composed of a long glass-topped table that seems smaller than it really is, plus scaled-down rust upholstered chairs on chrome bases. All these pieces have a floating, light-as-air look and help to visually expand space.

This den had small dimensions as did the other rooms: it is only 8' x 11'. Wall space was badly broken up by windows and there was an unattractive exposed radiator.

Interior designer Elroy Edson used the same basic neutral color scheme here. Pale cream wall-to-wall carpet stretches floor space, while cream, brown and gold wall covering in a contemporary pattern helps to create an open, airy look on the walls. A feeling of height is also introduced through the striped background effect of the wall covering. Windows now virtually disappear into the background because of their unobtrusive cream curtains. All the furniture was chosen with an eye towards a future move to a larger house. The saw-horse dining table now works as a desk and the sectional seating unit now turns a corner, while it will later be a conventional 90" sofa. The designer removed the tall exposed radiator and replaced it with a smaller one. This becomes a decorative and functional plus, covered by a unit that builds in both work surface and file cabinet.

PROBLEM: *Need to create a small desk-work area in an apartment already furnished and lacking the available space.*

SOLUTION: *Utilization of wall-hung furniture on a short wall in the foyer.*

Every inch counts in apartment living and the walls are a good place to find a little extra. Here, a very short wall in a entry foyer is put to work with walnut bookshelves and a cabinet desk. Because there are no legs to clutter the floor, wall-hung furniture creates an even greater sense of space. The drop-leaf desk front can be closed to be out of the way when not in use. The flexibility of the system allows shelves and units to be hung anywhere on the wall rails, to vary the arrangement or to accommodate extra pieces. Office-type carpet in this easy maintenance apartment is hard-wearing man-made fiber. Its small-scale pattern helps to expand space still further by being used wall-to-wall throughout.

4 · How to Revitalize a Tired Room

Often a room suffers from the blahs and has a tired look because it has not been redecorated for a long time. Of course not everyone can afford to redo a room every year or so, or replace furniture and furnishings. However, you can give any room a whole new appearance by revitalizing it, and this does not have to cost a fortune.

There are a variety of ways to bring fresh, beautiful looks to any room, whatever its basic problem. A room might suffer from any one of a number of ailments, but once you have put your finger on this you can easily correct it with a few clever decorating tricks.

A room may appear to be tired and dull because the walls and paintwork are grubby, the floor coverings worn and fabrics faded. Or the room might lack luster because there is little color, no visual excitement from accessories, or no focal point to give it a center of eye interest. Some rooms seem jaded simply because the furniture has been arranged in a haphazard manner and is thus without cohesion. Often the furniture itself has seen better days. But even this does not necessarily have to be discarded. It can be revamped with paint, new finishes and new upholstery materials. In fact, each one of the problems you might encounter has a solution and it is challenging, quite often lots of fun, to give a room new dimensions and make it more comfortable and attractive to live in, by using your own ingenuity.

Your basic tools are paint, wallpaper or other wall coverings, floor coverings and area rugs, fabrics, accessories and plants. A metal coil-spring tape measure, graph paper and a notebook will also come in useful if you have to measure the room, the furniture or both, and make a floor plan. This is always obligatory if you want to create new furniture arrangements or find a suitable wall for the creation of a focal point.

Your initial step is to analyze the room and pinpoint the actual reason for its tired overtones. It could be one thing or several. For instance, sometimes faded or limp draperies, a grubby window shade or some other type of poor window treatment is introducing an unattractive element into the room. If this is so, a spanking new treatment may be all you require to give a room a lift.

On the other hand, drab walls may be casting a pall over the entire area of space; in the same vein, worn or faded carpeting can destroy the overall effect. Fresh paint or wall covering, a new floor covering or an area rug will immediately update the room and also help to show furniture off to an advantage.

Sometimes it is the furniture itself that is destroying the appearance of the room. Wood furniture that is marred or scratched will detract from the most beautiful background; however, this can be treated to fresh paint or finishes that even the novice do-it-yourselfer will not find hard to handle. Slipcovers can be used to hide faded upholstery and this is often cheaper than having pieces reupholstered. Then again, a room may be dull simply because it has not been well accessorized.

Let's examine all the elements that help to give a tired room an uplift and look at some of ideas for using them effectively.

ENLIVEN WITH ACCESSORIES

All manner of accessories can be utilized to create a sparkling facade in any dull room in your home. Apart from the fact that they introduce color, life, movement and textures, they also add that very individual look that says something about you and your personal taste and interests.

Paintings, prints, posters, sculpture, ornaments, books, cushions and plants are some of the items which are readily available today and they don't necessarily have to cost a great deal. If you happen to have a creative hobby, such as needlework or crafts, the things you make yourself can also be utilized to introduce a very personal touch in a room. Needlepoint and gros point pillows and wall hangings are particularly effective, since they bring color, pattern and texture to seating and the walls.

Any dull wall immediately springs to life when it is treated to a grouping of pictures or other wall accessories. The grouping can be large or small depending on the size of the wall, but it needs to be carefully planned for the best effect. There are certain rules for hanging pictures and you should always bear these in mind.

1. Do not hang anything until you have the entire grouping assem-

bled, so that you know exactly what has to be included in the available space.

2. Before banging nails into the wall, group the pictures on the floor directly in front of the wall where they will be hung. Rearrange the paintings until you have the most effective grouping. You will then avoid making mistakes and damaging the walls.

3. Never hang pictures in a straight line, side by side and/or above and below each other. This is boring and banal.

4. Hang the pictures at different levels for movement and real balance.

5. Use pictures of various sizes and in different frames to create a change of visual pace.

6. Always be sure that the colors used in the paintings or prints blend with each other; wildly contrasting color tones can be extremely harsh and jarring to the eyes. The colors in the pictures should also be compatible with the color scheme of the room.

7. Always start with a major picture of a good size and hang this either to one side or in the center. Build the rest of the arrangement around this.

8. Be sure that your final grouping is in balance with the furniture placed against the wall below the grouping.

By paying attention to these few points you will be able to create an effective arrangement of pictures that does much to enhance the room.

Mirrors do a lot for a wall and a room. They introduce dimension and depth, reflect light and add sparkle. When you use a mirror on a wall always be sure it reflects attractive images. The effect is lost when the mirror simply reflects a blank wall. Place it strategically, so that it picks up reflections of such things as flowers, plants, accessories or furniture arrangements.

Interior designer Leif Pedersen has created some brilliant effects through the use of mirrors and candles. One of his most eye-catching ideas is composed of tall white candles in candlesticks of various heights, arranged on a console table or other small table in front of a large mirror or mirrored wall. He uses about a dozen candles, sometimes more, and places the tallest candles at the back closest to the mirror, the smaller ones towards the front of the grouping. The images are doubled and seem to stretch into infinity, for a sparkling, almost magical effect. This idea can be used in a living room, dining room or foyer.

Interior designer John Elmo often uses brackets and ornaments to dress up a tired wall. The brackets, generally of period style, are painted white or a color that blends with the walls. Each one is given a colorful ornament or object of art. A medium-sized wall will hold about six brackets comfortably; they should be carefully placed and hung for a well-balanced look. For a change of visual pace, John often selects brackets of varying sizes to hold both large and small objects.

I utilized this idea in my own dining room to turn one wall into a center of visual interest. I had the antique brackets painted white to blend with the green and white wallpaper, and most of the objects I have used on the brackets are white, yellow or pale green. To introduce splashes of more vivid color on the wall, I hung antique English plates made of glazed pottery in between the brackets.

All kinds of small decorative objects can be assembled on table tops for needed color and a play of diverse textures and shapes in a room. This idea is a quick and easy way of revitalizing a room that looks dreary and limp and it can be done on a relatively small budget. Small decorative accessories don't have to be expensive objects or priceless works of art. They can be items you have picked up on your travels or things you have found in the foreign import shops, thrift or junk shops. Your most important consideration is to use accessories that are colorful, attractive and, whenever possible, unique or different.

Ideal accessories to use on end, side or coffee tables are small snuff boxes, porcelain figurines, bowls of china flowers, small silver items, crystal objects, marble or onyx eggs and mineral specimens. The latter have become very popular in recent years and are most effective when grouped together for a mingling of colors and shapes.

Refurbishing a tired room with accessories can often be the beginning of a hobby you will find absorbing and lots of fun. Decide on a given object and start hunting it out to make a well-rounded collection. You have a limitless range to choose from—glass paperweights, small boxes made of silver, enamel or porcelain, antique letter seals, obelisks, shells and the mineral specimens mentioned before. All of these accessories usually look their best when they are displayed on a table which also holds a lamp, so that they are well illuminated.

If you have a collection of photographs of family and friends, look for unusual old frames and use these to frame the photographs. You can create an interesting grouping on a table, especially with ornate Victorian or Edwardian frames which you can readily find in second-hand shops. Alternatively, use fabric-covered frames mingled with others made of silver and leather. The secret is to utilize lots of photographs so that the grouping has impact on the table.

A dull corner in a tired room can be sparked up with an etagere which has been filled with interesting accessories. The etagere can be made of

115

wood, metal, plastic or steel and glass, whichever you prefer and can afford, and it makes an eye-catching display unit. The accessories should be varied in size, shape and color, and for additional interest, it's often a good idea to use several plants, preferably ferns which are light and airy in feeling.

Plants in themselves are a marvelous accessory for a tired room, particularly when you create a large grouping of diverse kinds. They can be used to dress up a dull corner, a tired wall or a window area, displayed on a unit such as a baker's rack or on small tables of varying heights. Ceiling-hung plants are also very effective and when used with a floor grouping they introduce a garden look indoors.

Shelves of books in colorful jackets do wonders for a tired room and also add a more furnished look, while handsome art books spark up a coffee table and pinpoint your personal interests. Pedestals holding pieces of sculpture can be highly dramatic and a handsome addition to a room, especially when they are highlighted with a small spotlight.

PROBLEM: *A modern room that looked cold and uninviting with its plain white walls and a neutral, solid-colored rug; also small fireplace looked unbalanced on the long wall.*

SOLUTION: *Utilization of colorful paintings and an area rug for warmth; plus lamp, accessories and plants for decorative finishing touches.*

In spite of the fact that this room was nicely furnished with modern pieces it had a cold look, mainly due to the stark white walls. However, adding to the cool, colorless feeling was a beige, flat-woven rug that did little for the room as a whole. The large rug, which covered up most of the floor in front of the fireplace, was removed and replaced with a handsome area rug. The free-flowing horizontal bands of the rug echo the geometric lines of the sofas, but in a soft manner, muting the rigidity. The owners found this an inexpensive and easy way to personalize the room and give it more warmth. The sculptured multi-dimensional rug has a shaggy high pile and a smooth low pile which introduces a much-needed contrast of textures in the area. A bright yellow and white painting splashed with red was cleverly hung at an angle, and it not only serves to brighten the wall but highlights the fireplace as well. In combination with the rug it also adds definition to the fireplace area and gives more importance to the small fireplace. Two small prints balance a small end table, as do the floor lamp and a vase of tall flowers; a plant was placed at the other end of the wall, again for balance and visual interest. Mineral specimens on the small table and the hearth are interesting pieces that bring color and shape to the white wall, while a collection of pillows warms up the leather sofas and introduces textural play.

PROBLEM: Unattractive, old-fashioned bathroom, marred tiled walls and an ugly window.

SOLUTION: Removal of tiles, use of wallpaper and an old stained-glass window for updated, sleek look.

Badly chipped, worn old tiles halfway up the walls surrounding the bath gave this bathroom a desolate look, while soaring dimensions added an unbalanced feeling in relation to the small floor area. An old-fashioned window was ugly and difficult to treat effectively and this added to the tired appearance. For this revamp, the tiles were removed and the walls were covered with vinyl wall covering in a large-scale pattern in light, sunny colors. The sturdy wall covering hides the poor walls and is highly practical since it is engineered to withstand steam and moisture. The large-scale pattern helps to diminish the soaring proportions and its airy look helps to push walls out, creating a sense of balance in the area. The wall covering was also used on the ceiling to pull it down by visual illusion and for continuity. An old stained-glass window, found in a junk shop, was an inexpensive buy that cleverly conceals the ugly window as well as an unattractive outside view. To cheer up the vanity, inserts of the wall covering were used on the doors. A few attractive accessories and new bath towels completed the revamp that gave an old room new dimensions.

PROBLEM: *Dull window treatment composed of old shutters; worn upholstery on chairs and ottoman; a damaged mahogany end table.*

SOLUTION: *Removal of shutters and installation of a fresh window treatment; new slipcovers; table-cloths for old table.*

Two sets of louvered shutters in a mahogany tone were too dark and heavy for this small window in a bedroom and actually detracted from the room's appearance. Worn slipcovers on the chairs and ottoman added a shabby look, while a stained and scratched end table seemed destined for the junk pile. Interior designer Ann Heller brought fresh new looks to the room that gave it an immediate uplift without costing a fortune. The designer removed the louvered shutters and replaced them with one set of open-fronted, fold-in shutters bought from a lumber yard. These she painted white and finished with tiny shirred curtains made of a remnant of fabric that matches the wallpaper. A left-over piece of wallpaper was used to cover the tiny valance made from a small piece of plywood. The designer then attached a window shade to round out the treatment and produce the necessary privacy. The yellow shade was trimmed with a floral border, cut out of extra paper, and was hem-shaped and gimp-trimmed to echo the traditional flavor of the overall decor. This combination of shade and shutters is decorative, practical, and creates a much lighter effect at the windows. Medium-priced green polka-dot fabric was turned into slipcovers that hide the faded upholstery on the chairs and ottoman and also introduce extra color and pattern play into the room. Instead of throwing out the damaged mahogany end table, as the owner had planned, the designer transformed it into a whole new table. A cheap unfinished wood circular top was attached to the table with screws and the whole was camouflaged with two home-made table-cloths. The under-cloth is light green, the top one made from the polka-dot fabric. This economical treatment actually made the table more practical, since the circular top provides much more space for a lamp and accessories.

119

PROBLEM: Drab walls and floor; haphazard furniture arrangement; ungainly windows made more conspicuous by two different treatments.

SOLUTION: Paint, wall-to-wall carpeting, shutters and a new bedspread; rearrangement of furniture.

This one-room studio apartment was furnished with pieces of wicker furniture and junk shop buys by its young occupant. After six months she found its drabness and lack of comfort depressing. The white walls were grimy and the haphazard furniture arrangement and scattered rugs broke up space and contributed to the cluttered feeling. Windows of disproportionate sizes were made more apparent by the different treatments. In general it was a limp, tired-looking room.

The revitalization of the room began with a paint job. The young owner and a friend painted the walls and ceiling a soft yellow that at once introduced sunny overtones and helped to create a more spacious look. Curtains and old shutters were removed and replaced with new matching shutters of unfinished wood, an inexpensive purchase from a lumber yard. These were painted the same yellow as the walls. They permit sunlight to fill the room while maintaining privacy and concealing the awkward air conditioner. They also introduce much-needed unity to the window wall. The major purchase for the studio apartment was the wall-to-wall carpeting, but even this was a budget-wise buy since it was a moderately priced product which comes in fifty stock colors. Lush jade green was the color chosen and it helps to emphasize the garden mood of the room. Tufted entirely of soil-hiding nylon it comes with the manufacturer's five-year guarantee and is as practical as it is colorful. It introduces a smooth, flowing feeling, helps to expand space visually and adds lots of comfort, warmth and insulation underfoot. The bed was left in the same position as before, but was refreshed with a quilted spread in bright greens and yellows on white, plus lots of colorful cushions. It now acts as a seating unit. The white wicker chair was refurbished with white paint and new cushions and partnered with a small wicker table, an inexpensive buy from a novelty store. This holds the white ginger lamp which was previously positioned in another area of the room. To soften the straight lines of the window wall, lots of plants were hung at various levels from the ceiling, reinforced by more plants on the floor. Two old mirrors were refinished and rehung on the wall above the bed, and this pair was turned into a decorative focal point with the addition of smaller mirrors found in a second-hand shop. Such things as the old bookcase and bentwood rocker were updated with white paint and placed at the opposite end of the room; also in this area (not shown in picture) are a dining table and chairs, all bought in an unfinished state and treated to white lacquer finish.

CHEER UP A ROOM WITH FABRICS

Fabrics can be utilized in a variety of ways to bring an updated uplift to a tired room short on color, liveliness and decorative interest.

For instance, they are marvelous for hiding cracked, marred or dirty walls or those covered with a faded and worn wallpaper. They are simply stretched from floor to ceiling and stapled into position at the top and bottom, or are attached with a special adhesive.

Interior designer Jane Victor likes to cover walls with shirred fabric for the soft yet rich look this introduces. She especially recommends this idea for a bedroom, dining room or a young girl's room where you want to hide poor walls or any odd architectural elements. But of course the idea can be utilized in any room which needs extra design interest or a little fillip.

This does not have to be a costly project if you use an inexpensive fabric, such as cotton, twill, synthetic materials or blends of cotton and synthetic fibers. The fabric must always be shirred first to fit each wall; then it can be attached with small nails or a staple gun. If the nails or staples show, Jane hides them with a narrow braid trim attached with adhesive or narrow strip molding. The shirred walls retain their freshness if they are periodically vacummed with the brush attachment of your regular vacuum cleaner.

Sometimes this same designer uses fabric on a ceiling and then repeats it in another area of the room, perhaps for draperies, slipcovers, on a bed or for a skirted table. The walls are painted in a color picked from the fabric for a coordinated look. This idea solves the problem of replastering or repainting a marred or cracked ceiling, while helping to introduce a custom-designed effect. The fabric is tacked or glued to the ceiling with a special adhesive and it is not a costly job, depending mainly on the price of the fabric you select.

Leif Pedersen suggests hiding poor walls by upholstering them. This technique also does much to uplift a drab room and it introduces a handsome, rich effect. It is not difficult to do yourself. The walls are first covered with inexpensive cotton wadding, which is tacked into position. The fabric is then stretched over this and also tacked down, the tacks hidden by strip molding or braid which is glued onto the fabric. Leif usually selects an inexpensive fabric of medium weight and a close weave, preferably in a solid color. The padded effect brings a custom-designed feeling to the room and also adds soundproofing and insulation. It works well in any room, other than a kitchen or bathroom of course.

Gloria Vanderbilt was one of the first designers to put fabric down on the floor, not as impractical an idea as it sounds. Once the fabric has been glued into position it must be treated to at least four to six coats of polyurethane varnish. This protects the fabric and adds long-lasting durability as well as a slick sheen. Don't ever use a fabric on the floor without adding the varnish finish.

You can create some really eye-catching effects in any room by carrying coordinated fabrics onto the walls and the furniture and to the windows, but they must harmonize with the fabric-covered floor. Some of Gloria Vanderbilt's schemes have included a mélange of patchwork and quilt patterns, mixes of floral and authentic period designs, all from her own fabric collections now being sold in the stores. However, you can evolve your own mixes, using geometrics, plaids, stripes, trellis and backet-weave patterns, whatever appeals to you and is suitable for the room. The only point to bear in mind is that they should be color matched and of similar scale so that they do not clash.

Certainly using fabric on the floor is an inexpensive way to rejuvenate a room that has limp overtones, and it is relatively easy to do yourself. Always be certain the fabric is stretched tightly from wall to wall and make sure there are no bubbles underneath from the glue. It is an ideal decorating technique for a bedroom, a guest room or a dining room.

Faded or worn upholstery on sofas and chairs introduces a shabby look into any room. If reupholstering them is too prohibitive in price, you can have slipcovers made for much less and they do the job of revamping furniture extremely well. You can also buy ready-made slipcovers for certain pieces, but be certain you have measured your furniture accurately to get the right size for the best fit.

If you cannot afford to reupholster or add new slipcovers, you can often camouflage worn upholstery by adding lots of cushions. But whether upholstery is worn or not, most sofas and large chairs require cushions to give them a finished look. Cushions introduce both color and textural play and so help to spark up both tired upholstery and a tired room, particularly one very low on bright color.

If your seating pieces are upholstered with a patterned fabric, it is best to select pillows in plain fabrics which harmonize with the colors in the pattern. When the upholstery fabric is plain you can go the other way and utilize patterned fabrics for the cushions. A variety of different textures produce extra visual interest and you can mix wools, velvets, silks, tweeds and cottons along with needlepoint and gros point pillows. If you enjoy needlework use your own creations to add a really individual look to seating pieces.

Here are some other ways to use fabric to revitalize a drab room.

• Cover a three-panel screen with an unusual fabric and place it in a lost corner or blank spot in a room.

• Cover two three-panel screens with a fabric matched to upholstery and place one at each side of a window in place of draperies.

• Give a circular unfinished wood table a floor-length cloth, made of a fabric that coordinates with upholstery or draperies, and use it for a lamp table or to display accessories.

• Frame a geometric or floral print and hang it on a wall instead of a painting.

• Hang fabric on a panel track to conceal a poor window or simply to enliven a dull wall.

• Hang a panel of fabric behind a bed in place of a headboard or behind a sofa as a backdrop for a painting or wall brackets holding ornaments or a collection of plates.

PROBLEM: *Tired bedroom with worn fabric canopy and spread on four-poster; worn upholstery on sofa; lack of accent color in neutral room.*

SOLUTION: *Utilization of sheets on bed and for upholstery of sofa; color introduced with paintings and plants.*

Although this bedroom had a light, airy feeling because of the all-cream scheme and the window and dressing-table treatments, it missed out a little on its decorative potential. The owner realized that the cream scheme was too bland as it stood; she also recognized that faded fabric on the bed and worn upholstery on the sofa introduced a slightly shabby look. Interior designer Dan Carithers came up with a two-fold solution; sheets utilized for bed cover and canopy, also sofa slipcovers; plants and paintings for a flash of color accents on the window wall. The designer had an eye for practicality as well as beauty and used the cotton-blend sheets to decorate off the bed, as well as on. Not only are they washable, but they provide more fabric for less money, especially extra-wide sheets, than yard goods bought at the sew-at-home counter. One sheet was stretched across the top of the bed for the actual canopy, held in place by hooks and rings in each corner. Another large sheet was cut in half and turned into side draperies, while two more were quilted to make a comforter. Along with matching sheets and pillowcases the bed takes on a custom-made look. Coordinated slipcovers refurbish the sofa that concealed good lines beneath beat-up upholstery. A print and a painting were hung on the walls on either side of the window and immediately introduced much-needed color. Final fillip were the many plants hung in the window area from the ceiling and placed on the floor.

PROBLEM: *Dull corner of a kitchen used for dining, with little space for extra furnishings.*

SOLUTION: *Various shades of red and orange paint for L-shaped corner walls; wall-hung furniture; accessories, plants and new color-coordinated draperies.*

This "eat-in" corner of a family kitchen was dull and unattractive. White walls created a nondescript look and there was very little floor space to include furniture other than the dining table and chairs. Designers Harry Schule and John McCarville set about dressing up the corner, first by painting the L-shaped corner walls in alternate panels of different shades of orange and red. They then added wall-hung furniture composed of shelves and cabinets. These are entirely functional yet help to bring a living room look to the "Cinderella" kitchen. The cabinet and drawers provide storage facilities while the shelves supply plenty of display space. All manner of attractive kitchen accessories introduce decorative overtones, along with plants, so that the corner takes on a wholly new appearance. The designers treated the window to light-weight draperies, color-coordinated to the red orange walls. The wall-hung furniture system in oiled walnut is ideal for a situation where shelves may need to be moved or added to.

PROBLEM: *Drab feeling in a living room, created by worn olive green wall-to-wall carpeting and dull olive and gold upholstery fabrics.*

SOLUTION: *Removal of old carpet; refinishing of floor and the addition of a colorful area rug; utilization of pillows for color.*

Dull olive green wall-to-wall carpeting, which was also somewhat worn, created a drab look in this living room. The feeling was emphasized by the olive and gold upholstery fabrics on the sofa and chairs. The owners could not afford to totally redecorate or have furniture reupholstered. After analyzing the room as a whole, they decided to redo the floor only, since the carpet was old and the main contributor to the drab mood. Removal of the carpeting revealed a good wood floor which was stained a dark mahogany and polished. An attractive rug was purchased for the area in front of the fireplace and it introduced a raft of bright colors which also relate to those already in the room. The shaggy texture of the rug is an added warming factor, providing contrast to the smooth surface of the exposed wood floor. A collection of pillows was used on the olive sofa to add color accents. Since the pillows were homemade and the floor refinished by the owners, the major purchase was the area rug. Even so, this revamp was done on a small budget.

PROBLEM: An all-white kitchen which had a cold and sterile appearance.

SOLUTION: Red and brown vinyl tiles laid down on the floor in a custom-design effect, reiterated by color-coordinated supergraphics carried up the door and wall and across the ceiling.

The galley-like feeling of this long, narrow kitchen was emphasized by the all-white color scheme. Although the kitchen had been expertly planned down to the last detail and was the ultimate in efficiency, it had a sterile ambiance. Since cabinets and equipment virtually filled all the wall space, it seemed hard to revitalize with color and accessories on the walls. Kitchen designer William Ketchum had the idea of treating the floor and the ceiling with vivid rafts of color to add warmth and decorative impact. Plain white floor tiles running down the center of the kitchen were removed and replaced with red vinyl tiles, square in shape but set diamond-wise for more effectiveness. These were flanked by narrow white tiles and then by brown tiles, arranged in a zigzag effect. The floor design was cleverly repeated up the door and wall and across the ceiling, for total coordination and an eye-catching look. The design on the door, wall and ceiling was simply painted on with lacquer paints which repeat the colors on the floor. The supergraphics do much to alleviate the confined feeling of the galley-like shape while dressing up the sterile white.

REVITALIZE A WILTING FLOOR

A floor obviously takes the most wear and tear in general living areas, especially when traffic is heavy. Replacing an entire floor covering is not always convenient or feasible, especially when cost factors are a major consideration.

A badly worn, spotted or faded wall-to-wall carpet destroys the look of a room, as does a scuffed wood or vinyl floor, even when all the other furnishings are in perfect condition.

One simple yet effective way to revitalize a wilting floor is to put down an area rug. An area rug can do a lot for a room as a whole. It immediately introduces color, pattern and texture and so distracts the eye from worn or faded areas; it also camouflages worn patches when correctly placed. Apart from this, an area rug can be cleverly utilized to pull a furniture arrangement together, demarcate specific areas within the room and direct traffic lanes.

The type of area rug you select depends of course on the overall decorative style of the room. If you have used traditional furniture it is safest to select a traditional area rug with a solid ground and a border, or either a Persian or Oriental rug. Some modern rugs do work in a traditionally furnished room, providing the design of the rug is not too contemporary. In a modern room you would be best advised to use a modern area rug, although in some instances you can introduce a striking effect by putting down an Oriental. When furnishings are somewhat eclectic you can utilize either a traditional or contemporary rug. Long-haired rugs, such as the Flokati, work well in rooms of almost any decorative style. Always be sure that the area rug you select is color-matched to the room, so that it blends harmoniously with the overall scheme or adds just the right color accents.

Generally you can safely use an area rug on top of an existing floor, providing this is not too badly damaged. However, before adding the rug it's a good idea to clean up the existing floor covering. For example, wall-to-wall carpeting should be shampooed and a vinyl floor should be thoroughly cleaned and rewaxed. If you are putting the area rug on top of a scuffed wood floor, clean and repolish the wood first. When an existing floor covering is very badly worn or faded, it may be necessary to remove this completely. But before pulling up carpeting, vinyl or any other type of floor covering, make sure you have a decent wood floor underneath, which can be stained and polished. As a safety measure anchor an area rug into position with non-skid tapes, to prevent slips and falls.

If you have a wilting wood floor you can either have it refinished in the traditional dark colors, or you can do something more up-to-date with paint. White and light-colored painted floors are currently very popular and they do much to enliven a room and open up the floor area for a feeling of extra spaciousness. When floors are painted, they should also be sealed and protected with several coats of clear polyurethane varnish. You can cover the entire floor with a pale paint and leave it at that, or you can decorate the pale background with a stenciled design for extra decorative interest. Special kits for doing this are available at art shops and you can add either a simple border or an all-over design, depending on your personal tastes. Light painted floors are practical even in very heavy traffic areas, once they have been protected with the polyurethane finish. They are durable, don't scuff or soil easily and are simple to clean when they do get grubby.

If you are bored with wall-to-wall carpets, area rugs and wood floors, vinyl is an alternative that does much to enliven a drab room. This resilient floor covering is now available in an amazing number of patterns and colors and it can be cleverly used to create a custom-designed look underfoot. Many of the patterns simulate old tiles, leather, brick, planking, marble, ceramic and parquet. Whichever one you choose, be sure it is suitable for the period and style of the furniture you have used in the room.

PHOTO ON FOLLOWING PAGE

PROBLEM: Tired look created by worn vinyl-tiled floor and faded draperies.

SOLUTION: Addition of a rich-looking wall-to-wall carpet and a custom-designed window treatment.

The handsome look of this study was slightly diminished by worn vinyl tiles on the floor and faded floor-to-ceiling draperies that had seen better days. Interior designer Leona Kahn decided to give the room an immediate uplift by putting down rich-looking carpet that also adds extra comfort underfoot. The designer also dispensed with dust-catching draperies altogether and in their place used a handsome, custom-designed window treatment. This is composed of a wood lambrequin and light sheer curtains which wash easily. The lambrequin gets its custom look from the carpet used to decorate it. These were leftover pieces from the floor and were glued onto the lambrequin, which is finished with molding on the edges. The treatment is highly practical since it simply vacuums as easily as the curtains wash. It is also simple for a do-it-yourselfer to design and build; alternatively it can be made by a carpenter and is not an expensive project.

PROBLEM: *Bland, banal-looking room created by too many neutral colors plus natural wicker furniture, natural matchstick blinds, straw rug and natural wood furniture.*

SOLUTION: *Use of colorful paint and wall covering, plus gaily patterned cotton for upholstery.*

This living room was comfortable but lacked any visual excitement because of a very bland color scheme based on lots of neutral colors. Walls were beige, while most of the furniture was in natural tones with beige upholstery. Even the straw rug reiterated the no-color look. To give the room bright, sunny overtones decorator Alfred Ferraro splashed vivid yellow paint over two walls and the ceiling; a third wall was covered with bright red wall covering spotted with matching yellow. Window frames and wall and ceiling beams were also painted yellow. Into this sparkling shell, the designer introduced a raft of reds and blues in cotton fabrics used for upholstery and the screen. They add vibrancy and life, and work well with the yellow walls and natural wicker furniture. A cheerful patchwork cotton shows up on the sofa, while stripes make a strong statement on the screen and floor cushions; solid yellow cotton duck tailors effectively into a cushion for the scoop chair and for the tablecloth. Blue corduroy velvet used to slipcover a chair picks up the exact blue of a cotton cushion on the sofa. This mélange of gay colors helps to highlight the natural tones of furniture, matchstick blinds and the straw rug, which had previously been lost in the room.

PROBLEM: *Dark, unattractive bathroom with lacquered brown walls, no windows and an awkward step-up to bath; general lack of space emphasized by color scheme.*

SOLUTION: *Utilization of wallpapers with shiny surfaces; bright green carpet remnants to enliven floor; addition of a large mirror and plants.*

Like most apartment bathrooms this one was small and dark since it had no windows. Emphasizing the confined feeling were walls lacquered brown and a brown vinyl-tiled floor. An odd step-up to the bath was an awkward element that created an unbalanced look. The owner realized the easiest way to cheer up the room was to get rid of the brown color scheme which was so overpowering. To repaint would have been very costly, since lots of coats would have been necessary to cover up the brown; so instead the owner decided to hide the paint with wall covering. He selected two different ones, but both were related by their shiny reflective surfaces. He used a solid silver vinyl in the bath area, which immediately opened up the area; his choice for the rest of the room was a silver and green light-patterned wall covering, also a hardy vinyl which withstands steam and moisture. This stripe pattern helps to push walls out for a feeling of extra space. Since it would have been expensive to totally redo the floor, small inexpensive remnants of a light green shag carpet were bought and used to cover the step up and for a small area rug in front of the vanity. Apart from adding lively color to the brown floor the carpet provides comfort underfoot. A large traditional mirror with a silver-painted frame was used in place of a much smaller one; this too helps to lighten the room and make it appear less cramped. Plants added a touch of greenery, while glass accessories dress up the vanity.

REVAMP OLD FURNITURE

Sometimes a room has a weary look because the furniture is old and worn. Obviously it is not always possible to discard this furniture and start again from scratch, buying lots of new pieces. And anyway, this is not always necessary. Many old wood pieces can be cleverly revamped and brought up-to-date through the use of paint, lacquer, antique finishes and some of the latest polishes.

If you cannot afford to send scratched and stained wood furniture out to be repolished, you can refinish it yourself quite easily today, and relatively cheaply. There are a variety of new products available that quickly hide stains and other surface marks and scratches with a protective film that has a high-gloss finish. Deep scratching and nicks can be camouflaged with a special spray-on product similar to furniture polish that fills out the dents and polishes at the same time.

Really badly damaged wood can be stripped down and antiqued with special products that come in pre-packed antiquing kits with detailed instructions. If this idea does not appeal to you, damaged wood can be stripped to its natural color and simply waxed.

Painted furniture is very popular today and it enhances a room and dispenses with its tired overtones at the same time. The most popular paints are those with a shiny lacquer finish, especially white, red and black. Chair frames lacquered white are a favorite with interior designers, since they do much to highlight fabrics. Any chair frame can be lacquered white, whether it is modern or period in design; old furniture particularly takes on a new look when it has been treated to white paint. Chests, end tables, consoles, coffee tables and even dining-room tables can all be lacquered successfully, and of course painted furniture is ideal for bedrooms.

If you cannot revamp a piece of furniture in the ways just mentioned and have to discard it, you can replace it with a budget-wise piece. For instance, unfinished wood furniture comes in all styles and it is easy to lacquer it yourself; alternatively you can use a piece found in a junk or thrift shop, which has been refinished with polish or paint. Badly marked wood coffee and end tables can be replaced with plastic or steel-and-glass pieces and these can be worked into traditional decorating schemes as well as those with more modern overtones. Floor-length cloths can also be used to hide old tables and help to introduce extra color accent and texture into that tired room.

Once you have revamped your old furniture and given it brand-new looks, consider the idea of rearranging it in fresh groupings. Often it is the actual arrangement of the furniture that has been producing a jaded mood in the room. For instance, furniture that straggles off in all directions produces a haphazard, untidy look; furniture that is packed tightly together in cramped groupings gives any room a cluttered, uncomfortable appearance. Analyze your furniture groupings to ascertain their validity for the room and its function, and when necessary regroup them. Or if you wish, simply rearrange furniture to give the room a whole new ambiance.

PROBLEM: *Old window treatment composed of faded blue draperies and a worn window shade which detracted from the overall handsome appearance; a lost corner next to the window which needed decorative overtones added.*

SOLUTION: *Fresh window treatment created from screens and plants; console table, lamp and accessories utilized in the corner.*

A handsome new sofa, chairs and a coffee table suddenly focused attention on the worn, faded window treatment in this living room, a situation that often occurs when new items are brought into an existing room. Since the owners had discarded quite a number of pieces of furniture to make room for the new larger pieces, a blank corner near the window stuck out like a sore thumb. This too needed to be dressed up for a finished look in the room. The owners began by removing faded floor-length draperies and a dirty, tired window shade. To add a slick tailored look at the windows, three-panel screens covered in an attractive fabric were utilized in place of the usual draperies. The screens add an architectural feeling and do not block out any of the actual window. For an unusual effect at the window itself, shelves were built and filled with plants. They introduce color and movement, yet allow light to filter into the room. Extra pieces of fabric, actually left over from the screens, were used to make pillows for the sofa and a larger one for floor seating. To fill out the blank corner wall, the owners added a console table in the same parquet wood design as the coffee table. This is an ideal spot for a lamp and accessories. An attractive print adds the finishing touch.

PROBLEM: *Banal feeling in a basement chiefly due to lack of architectural elements and windows, reinforced by walls painted white.*

SOLUTION: *Use of three wall coverings to create simulated paneling, shutters and draperies.*

The main problem with this basement family room was lack of architectural elements and windows. The unbroken expanse of wall area was dull and especially uninteresting because it was painted white. It provided no contrast for the white upholstered furniture blocks and so the overall mood was dull, cold and bare. The owner asked interior designer Peggy Walker to undertake the revitalization of the family room, which had to be done on a small budget. With this limitation, the designer knew she could not go to the expense of adding structural elements, such as beams or built-ins, to break up the expanse of wall space. Her solution was the use of three wall coverings that introduce that much-needed interest and bring definition to the wall areas at small cost. She selected shutter-patterned panels of vinyl wall covering for the back wall, which look like real shutters, have an opening-up effect and are downright deceptive, camouflaging the fact that the room has no windows. For realism and continuity, the designer covered the door in the adjoining corridor with the same wall covering. To simulate draperies and further break up wall space, she put up panels of bamboo-patterned wall covering in white, brown and silver. This also helps to anchor the seating arrangement and acts as a focal point at this end of the room. The vinyl wall coverings are fabric backed and are perfect for hiding marred walls; they are also easy to maintain, requiring only sponge-clean care. From this same collection Peggy Walker selected a third wall covering that looks like wood paneling to cover the rest of the walls.

5 · Formulas for Solving Color Problems

Color is undoubtedly one of the most exciting decorating elements. It not only creates a particular mood in a room, but it says a great deal about you and your personal tastes. It is also the first thing you notice when you enter a room, because it makes the strongest and most lasting impression.

A well-planned color scheme creates that necessary smooth backdrop for furniture and furnishings, and so does much to create real beauty in a room. But color is a magical decorating tool as well, since it has the ability to change the shape, size and overall dimensions, making space seem larger or smaller, depending on the actual colors used. It can be cleverly utilized to correct awkward shapes, camouflage architectural oddities or highlight a special architectural feature. Most importantly, color is the one great decorative unifier, blending unrelated objects together for a cohesive and harmonious whole.

Apart from all of these pluses, a good color scheme is budget wise, since it can give a room a more furnished look. In fact, clever color combinations often dispense with the need for lots of furniture. Remember that clear, bright colors cost no more than dull or drab ones; a can of bright yellow paint can be bought for the same price as a can of beige paint; and all the other color elements, such as floor coverings, wall coverings and fabrics, have no special price tag because of the interesting combinations of colors they feature.

Obviously, then, color is an asset in decorating, especially when you are working on a small budget or have to solve particular problems in a room, such as lack of space, too much space, awkward shapes or architectural defects. The illusions it creates can eliminate the need for certain furnishings or expensive structural changes. Whichever job you want to do, color is one of your best decorating friends. And yet many people are afraid of using color, probably because it is relatively easy to make mistakes by combining the wrong colors. Yet again, other people are timid with color, because they simply do not know *how* to go about building a successful color scheme.

139

FORMULA: Black and White plus a Vivid Color

Black and white creates a crisp look in any room, whatever its size or shape. This combination lives well over a long period of time because of the smooth, balanced feeling it introduces. However, black and white are neutrals that need enlivening by a vivid accent color if they are to look their best. It's an easy combination to work with because you are building from only two colors which work well together and so are not hard to handle. Once the two-color scheme is in place, pick a vivid accent shade and use it for furniture, accessories and art. Good accents with black and white are red, from brick to crimson, sharp greens, yellow, orange, bright blue, coral and purple. Generally it's a good idea to use more white than black over large expanses of unbroken space such as the walls, especially if the room is small. Both black and white work well on a floor, either alone or together.

This living room with a dining area draws its sophisticated look from the black and white scheme highlighted by silver and fire-engine red. The formula here is black and white in combination on the floor; black and silver in combination on the screens, with black, white, silver and red showing up in solid rafts throughout the room. The owner began with the floor, using black and white vinyl tiles to create a checkerboard effect. The tile pattern expands the floor space visually, while floor-length white draperies add to the feeling of space in the room. The walls in the living room (not shown) are white, and white upholstery fabric is used for the sofa; black balances this play of white-on-white, showing up in the coffee table and side chairs. Adding the necessary color fillip are a red end table, red accessories and red paintings on the wall. Dividing the room without diminishing the feeling of spaciousness are the tall screens, made of wood and covered with black and silver wallpaper in an open basket-weave pattern. This pattern and the reflective quality of the silver paper adds a light airy look to the tall screens. This airy mood extends beyond the screens into the dining area. Promoting the look are white and chrome director's chairs and a Parsons dining table covered with white and silver vinyl. The end wall painted bright fire-engine red adds the necessary flash of vivid color and also makes an excellent backdrop for the white and chrome furniture, lamp and silver painting.

Because it introduces a feeling of spaciousness, black and white is a good combination to use in a room filled with furniture, as illustrated in this all-purpose living room. Designer William Storey used a simple, easy to handle formula: an all-white shell highlighted by black and white light-scaled patterns with vivid yellow as the accent color. His adroit use of color helped to play down the cluttered look. Walls were painted white and the floor was covered with white vinyl. He then sparked up the dull window wall with a quintet of slim-lined shades made of black and white ticking laminated onto plain shades. Hung within the white frames, they distribute linear interest around the room and also counteract the horizontal bulk of the bookcases clustered along one wall. Sunshine-bright upholstery, which took its color cue from the facing on the storage units, leads the eye directly to the bold black and white houndstooth rug, establishing a pleasant balance of pattern and color. Touches of black and white in accessories highlight the yellow.

But these fears can easily be overcome, once you are aware of some of the special effects color creates. When you understand the principles of using color to its best advantage in a room, you will have that necessary self-confidence to go ahead and create beautiful, even highly different, visual effects in your home. The following points relating to color and its uses will serve as good guidelines when you are building a color scheme.

COLOR PLAYS TRICKS

It would be wrong to suggest that color does not play tricks, because it does and very often. In fact, in its hundreds of mutations, color can often create a mood or an effect that was not only unplanned but totally unexpected. This happens because color is capricious. Color actually *changes* under different conditions. It is worthwhile making a note of these different changes which occur, for future reference.

1. Color changes under varying light conditions, whether that light is natural or artificial.

2. Color takes on a different tone when placed next to another color.

3. Color undergoes an enormous change when used in a large expanse as compared to a small, concentrated mass.

Let us examine why these changes take place, so that you will fully understand how to handle color effectively and avoid making mistakes.

COLOR AND LIGHT   Color and light work together to create many different effects in a room. As I pointed out earlier, color is capricious and this is especially so under changing light conditions. This is because any light falling on any colored surface affects the appearance of that color. Light brings out the actual value of the color: sometimes it makes it seem brighter and warmer; conversely, certain light can make a color seem more subdued, dull and even cold.

These effects are created by artificial illumination as well as natural daylight. For this reason, it is always a good idea to check color samples in artificial light during the day and at night, as well as in natural daylight, in the room where the color will be used. This will help you to analyze the color and the effect it will create, and so prevent you from making mistakes which can be both costly and time-consuming to correct.

(See photographs on the next two pages.)

FORMULA: *One Strong Color Splashed Throughout a Room Highlighted by Contrasting Accent Colors*

One strong color splashed throughout a room can create a stunning, even dramatic, effect and it makes an ideal backdrop for furniture and accessories. A scheme based on a single color is easier to create than one built around many, as there is less chance of making bad mistakes by combining colors that don't blend well together. However, a strong color used over major areas of space needs to be highlighted by paler or lighter accent colors, which help to set it off so that it lives up to its potential. Strong colors which work well for a one-color scheme include bright red, chocolate brown, vivid blues and greens, rich corals and apricots and strong yellows.

Interior designer Michael Greer used chocolate brown as the dominant color in this stylish living room high on good taste and good looks. The designer took the dark brown over all four walls and up onto the ceiling to make a strong color statement in the room, and repeated it in the upholstery fabric used on the two antique chairs. To lighten the effect of the brown he used a cream carpet and cream fabric for the window treatment. The pale lemon yellow of the upholstery fabrics is a stunning and unusual color accent and it brings out the richness of the walls. A cream-colored painting echoes the color of the window treatment, while a Chinese lacquered screen is a superb piece on the main wall, introducing further color play and an eye-catching center of interest. Other color accents, which are kept to a minimum, are neutral metals and glass and a soft green which picks up the green from the carpet's border. Since brown absorbs light it needs these light colors for accents, as well as plenty of natural or artificial illumination in the room, if it is to work well.

In the same apartment Michael Greer introduced a lively change of color pace, again by utilizing a strong color. This time it is a sharp stringent green. The creme-de-menthe green appears in the entrance foyer leading into the brown living room. For total color cohesion the designer carried the green from the walls onto the doors and up onto the ceiling as well. The green is highlighted by dark brown molding and dados, accented by white candles in the silver wall sconces and white shades on the silver chandelier. The custom-made area rug cleverly carries the creme-de-menthe green onto the dark brown floor.

Interior designer Joan Blutter selected vibrant blue as the strong color for this scheme in a living room. She splashed it down onto the floor by way of the wall-to-wall carpeting and then took it up onto the windows and the back of the wall-length display cabinet. It also reappears at the far end of the room (not shown) in upholstery fabrics. To bring out the richness of the deep blue, the designer used pearly gray on the walls, the ceiling, for the woodwork of the cabinet and the upholstery on the wing chair. Touches of pale green are soft accents, while the deep blue crushed velvet on the back of the cabinet makes a rich backdrop for the red book bindings and green, white and blue porcelain. Since this is a cool color, the designer recommends it for use in rooms with a sunny, warm exposure.

Before you choose a color scheme for a room, it is important to ascertain the amount and intensity plus the direction of natural light coming into the room. You can easily do this by noting the number of windows, their size and the direction they face.

• Windows that face north or east bring cool light into the room.

• Windows with a southern or western exposure get direct sunlight more hours of the day and so fill the room with much warmer light.

• Cool colors such as green, blue and white will appear to be extremely cold in northern or eastern light.

• Warm colors, such as red, orange, coral and gold will look very hot and more intense in southern or western light.

It is just as important to consider the artificial light which will be used in a room. Before you settle on a color scheme analyze the amount of artificial illumination required and the actual number of lighting fixtures you will be using. The actual function of the room usually helps you to pinpoint this. For example, you will probably include more lamps in a living room than you would in a bedroom or dining room; kitchens and bathrooms also require plenty of lighting fixtures.

Artificial lighting should be carefully chosen to enhance a color scheme and both should be coordinated in the early planning stages of decorating or redecorating.

Make a note of the following types of lighting and special effects they create in a room.

• Incandescent lighting, which is very bright, usually adds a flattering and warming glow to a color scheme and creates a serene, harmonious effect.

• Low-wattage lighting tends to make colors look drab, sometimes much darker than they really are, because this is dull light. This should always be used in combination with other lighting.

• Fluorescent lighting, the type often found in kitchens and bathrooms, has the ability to change many colors completely. The actual effect varies, depending on the type of tube utilized. Generally, fluorescence creates a bluish or washed-out look. It seems best to avoid using this as direct lighting.

• Colored light created by the use of colored bulbs can be used to play up certain color schemes. The most popular are pink bulbs which introduce a soft glow into a room. These can be used with practically every color scheme.

(See photographs on the next two pages.)

Brilliant red creates a smashing effect in this living room designed by Michael Greer. His formula: red, red, red all the way for the utmost in dramatic impact. To this end he used it on the walls, the ceiling, the doors, for upholstery materials and drapery fabrics. It even makes a strong appearance in the antique rug. This lively all-red scheme was cooled by touches of pale cream in accessories; dark wood tones and dark marble in furniture and the mahogany-stained wood floor all add the necessary balance. Touches of gilt underscore the brilliant effect of the period room. Like brown, red absorbs light rays, and so requires lots of natural illumination and lamps in a room where it is used profusely.

Deep purple is the strong color used as a catalyst in this modern bedroom. Because it is such an intense color it was used on the floor, where it introduces impact and vibrancy without overpowering, as it would if utilized on the walls. The exact color of the wall-to-wall carpet is picked up in the fabric used for the draperies and the bedspread. Bright green, which also appears in the fabric, was chosen as the main accent color. It flashes across two walls and spices up the plastic desk chair. Since these two colors are dominant and vibrant they were cooled down by splashes of white—at the windows in the sheer curtains, in the lamp shade and the matting around the pictures. A white ceiling and white woodwork complete the cooling effect in a room full of lively color interest.

A deep shade of peach introduces a warm, rich glow into this living room designed by Michael Greer. Peach walls with a glazed effect are balanced by a peach ceiling and brocade draperies in an identical tone, for a smooth, colorful shell. The designer continued the peach throughout the rest of the room, in various deeper tones. It was utilized for the upholstery on side and arm chairs and the cushions on the green sofa. Even the carpet of a brickish tone has peach interwoven into the cream and green border. These three colors in muted tones also appear on the two tub chairs in the foreground. The one contrasting color accent in the room is the green sofa. Highlights are black and white, as seen in the vases and the lamps. Since peach is a warm color it is ideal for use in rooms with cold northern exposures.

147

148

COLOR AND COLOR   Color is always affected by its neighbor, and this is a vital point to bear in mind when selecting two or three colors to use together in one room. Any color takes on a different tone when it is placed next to another color. This happens because colors tend to bring out the *value* of each other. *Value* refers to a color's lightness and darkness. Obviously certain color combinations create stunning effects, while others introduce bad ones. Here are some examples.

• A dark color looks its best when used with a lighter color, which brings out its intrinsic, rich value. The darker color is effectively highlighted and brought into focus.

• A dark color placed next to another dark color will fail because the values of each individual color are too similar. A dull, drab effect is produced.

• A pale or light color looks and lives its best when highlighted by a darker or more vivid tone, again because values are properly balanced.

• A pale color in combination with another pale color loses its impact because their values are akin to each other. They produce a washed-out look.

• Two vivid colors together don't work well because of identical values. They are too intense together, fight each other and so introduce a jarring effect.

Visualize these two examples to understand the actual effects: *Brown* placed next to black, tan, purple, navy blue, fir green or gray looks too dark and heavy because it is missing out on its color potential. Yet brown partnered with lemon, coral, shrimp, peach, beige, pale blue or green suddenly comes alive and its richness and depth is underscored. *Deep blue* teamed with gold, gray, purple, brown, avocado or moss green seems to have no life, because these colors are too dark and dull to work with it well. However, deep blue highlighted with white, pale green and blue, yellow, red, orange, beige or shrimp suddenly produces sparkle because these tones give it that necessary lift.

COLOR AND QUANTITY   A color can look totally different, depending on the amount of space it covers. For instance, any color appears much brighter and more intense when it is used in quantity over a large expanse, such as the four walls of a room. The same color will look much less vivid when used in small doses, such as in a little room or on only one or two walls. For this reason it is important to view color samples very carefully before selecting one for an overall scheme. It is always a fairly safe idea to select a slightly less intense tone than you really want for walls, as this will still have that necessary brightness when it covers the entire area.

(See photographs on the next two pages.)

FORMULA: Use of Ready-made Sources to Build a Color Scheme—a Fabric, a Floor Covering or a Wall Covering

A color scheme which draws its inspiration from a ready-made source is most effective in any room, because it produces a feeling of true color coordination. It is also very easy to build a total scheme in this way, as you are utilizing colors already mixed and matched for the best results by color experts. Apart from simplifying the task of creating a successful color scheme, this method prevents ghastly mistakes with badly matched colors. The best ready-made sources to work with are fabrics, wallpapers or other wall coverings and floor coverings. Select the color from the source that pleases you the most and use this for major areas of space. Accent this color with one or two secondary colors, borrowed from the ready-made source.

This charming studio apartment aglow with warm colors took its entire scheme from a Chinese-inspired traditional fabric used for the alcove bed-sofa. Because this room has to live around the clock and serve a variety of functions, the owner wanted a soft restful shade for the background composed of walls, built-in units and doors. She selected the palest green in the fabric, a light apple, which also considerably expands the feeling of space in the dark room. With the apple green in place, she then selected another color from the attractive fabric for the floor. Her choice was the deep melon taken from the broad stripe. This rich tone adds just that necessary dash of strong color and helps to introduce warmth juxtaposed against the green. Her final selection for major items was the brilliant yellow of the background of the fabric. This was used on the two chairs, and also shows up in the painting and other small accessories. To color-tie the rest of the room to the bed-sofa area, the owner flashed extra fabric around the room, using it to skirt an unfinished wood table and to cover the ottoman. Pulling the whole scheme together for total color coordination are pillows in all the shades depicted in the fabric—green, melon, yellow and blue.

A scheme based on two colors is simple to put together, especially when the two colors are borrowed from a two-color wall covering. Interior designer Abbey Darer used this technique to create a cool restful look in this charming bedroom. Her ready-made source was the blue and white floral wall covering which comes with its own matching fabric. The designer utilized the two for a custom-designed look and total color coordination within the room. The wallpaper was used to cover the plain wood bedposts and to decorate the window seat, as well as for the walls. She then spread the matching fabric all over the room for a harmonious color-pattern mood. A large piece was shirred for the panel behind the bed; other lengths were turned into the quilted bedspread and the pillow shams. Remnants left over from these large pieces were utilized for upholstery on the built-in window seat, cushions for the chairs and shirred curtains on the window shutters. To fulfill the blue and white mood, the designer selected a deep blue wall-to-wall carpet and all white furniture and lamps. This technique for building a successful color scheme is particularly recommended for those who find it difficult to create color schemes or who are afraid of mixing lots of colors together.

COLOR AS A DECORATING TOOL

Color can create many illusions in a room and this is an important consideration when you are working on a limited budget or need to solve an architectural problem.

Some of the optical illusions color creates are given here; they will help you to plan color schemes successfully and assist you in solving your decorating problems.

ILLUSIONS OF SPACE   Clever use of the right colors will help you to introduce a feeling of space in a small or low-ceilinged room. The best colors to select to produce this optical illusion are light and pale colors. These colors appear to let the eye look "through and beyond," because they do not stop the eye. In actuality, they *recede* and so create the effect of pushing out walls.

Light or pale colors have another advantage that makes them ideal for use in a small room. They reflect light rays instead of absorbing them, again helping to further the sense of spaciousness. Light colors take advantage of all natural light and also help to make artificial lighting seem that much more effective.

In a low-ceilinged room you can introduce added height by painting the ceiling white or a pale color. This helps to make it soar upward. Underfoot, these same colors help to visually expand the floor space, by illusion of course, but it is a clever way of helping a room to grow in dimension. If you use light or pale colors in a large room, this too will appear to be more spacious than it actually is.

DIMINISHING SPACE   Certain colors can be utilized to help you diminish the size of the a large room, by optical illusion. Bright or strong colors work visual magic in reverse to the light tones.

Because they *advance* and stop the eye, they help to make a large area of space seem smaller. They create the effect of walls being pulled inward and so introduce more intimacy and warmth. Bright and strong colors tend to absorb light rays, and this effect underscores the warm mood and helps to reduce the dimensions considerably.

Bright, strong colors work particularly well in rooms that have cold, barnlike proportions or high, soaring ceilings. These visual illusions, created by either dark or light colors, do much to make a room live well and often help you to save money.

(See photographs on the next two pages.)

Here is another two-color scheme borrowed from a wallpaper, created for a living room by designer Abbey Darer. This time she has utilized a slightly different technique. The stylized trellis-like patterned paper was used on the walls to set the mood and then the designer borrowed the bright yellow from the paper and splashed it around the room in solid rafts. It is repeated in the upholstery materials, in the vinyl floor tiles and for some of the accessories. Staying within the two-color limits for the entire scheme, the designer selected the white of the paper's background for all other major areas of color. These are the pieces of wicker furniture, the fluffy area rug and the lamp shades, plus the window shutters. With the yellow-white scheme in place, the young designer decided the room needed just a little extra color fillip. To this end she used a yellow painting featuring crimson flowers. This too became a ready-made color source, since she picked up the crimson tones in the painting in a cushion and in the red tulips. To balance the color play she then added a profusion of green plants at the window. Use this formula for adding accent colors, if your two-color scheme needs an extra sprinkling of vivid color. The designer recommends this yellow-white color scheme for rooms that are dark, small or filled with cold light.

This floral fabric was the ready-made source selected by interior designer Virginia Frankel for a small living room. To introduce much-needed airiness into the confined space, the designer painted the walls white, the same color as the fabric's background. She then carried the dark blue in the pattern down onto the floor, by way of the wall-to-wall carpeting. White coffee tables and lamps repeat the white and help to promote the sparkling, fresh ambiance. Green, one of the other secondary colors in the fabric, was utilized for small accents, mainly fresh plants and the cushion on the sofa. Two paintings add just that light splash of color needed to introduce extra life and were carefully selected to harmonize with the strong floral. Since blue, white and green produce an extremely cool effect, Virginia Frankel suggests using it in rooms that get lots of sun or have a warm southern or western exposure. It's also an ideal scheme for stretching space by visual illusion.

Interior designer Jane Victor created an elegant blue and white scheme for this stylish bedroom in a New York apartment, using the handsome carpet as her ready-made source for the two major colors in the room. She took the navy blue of the carpet's background and toned it down to a slightly lighter shade for the walls and the ceiling. A very vivid blue, also a derivative of the navy blue carpet, was chosen for the velvet draperies, to upholster a stool and for the lacquer on the French desk. A sofa in the same blue (not shown) completes the color play in the window area of the room. Focal point of the room is the massive four-poster bed, Jane Victor's own design, which gains added attention because of the slightly raised platform it rests on. The designer lacquered this spanking-bright white to make it stand out against the dark blue walls and also to pick up the white stripe in the carpet. The crimson-bow pattern of the carpet introduces necessary accent color, and this crimson is picked up in small table-top accessories on the desk and a coffee table. When a strongly patterned carpet is used as a color source as this is, the designer recommends balancing it with plain walls and fabrics, to avoid an overly fussy effect created by too many patterns.

CORRECTING ARCHITECTURAL DEFECTS   It is easy to conceal architectural defects in a room through the use of one color or closely blended colors carried throughout. All closely blended colors are related to each other and so the eye moves smoothly across them, since it is not distracted by sharp contrasts. For example such things as an ugly fireplace, unsightly radiators and air conditioners, unattractive window frames, ceiling beams and other odd architectural details are unobtrusive when painted the same color as the walls. This is because they fade away into the background. The same effect can be created with woodwork when this too is painted the same color as the walls.

Then again, pale and strong colors can be combined in a room to correct architectural peculiarities. You can change the shape of a room very easily by utilizing this combination. Since pale or light colors *recede* and dark or strong colors *advance* all manner of interesting optical illusions can be produced.

One good example of this color technique is the way light and dark colors can be used to alter the shape of a long, narrow room with a corridor appearance. The idea is to make this type of room look square. It is accomplished by painting the two short end walls in the same bright color, the two longer side walls in a paler tone, related if possible for a harmonious look. The bright end walls will *advance* towards the center of the room, the pale side walls will *recede*, so that the room seems much less elongated, squarer, in fact, by illusion.

INTRODUCING A MOOD   Skillful use of color will introduce any mood you want in a room. Before you settle for a particular scheme, consider the mood you wish to create. Then analyze all the colors which will do this most effectively.

A Tranquil Mood is produced by all the soft, restful colors, such as pale blue, pale green, pale yellow, white, light peach or apricot, all the beige and sand tones, pearl gray and lilac.

A Dramatic Mood is created by strong, intense colors, like red, bright blue, purple, orange, emerald green, hot coral and brown.

A Cool Mood springs from light airy blues, greens, and white; combinations of these colors laced with white; and black and white.

A Sunny Mood is produced by sunny yellows, oranges, shrimp, rich peach and light apple green, and combinations of these with white.

A Warm Mood is built from all the hot colors from the spectrum, such as red, orange, gold, terra cotta, purple, and all the earthy autumnal colors.

*FORMULA: Borrow Nature's Colors from Spring through Winter and Utilize
Them in Basic Two-color Schemes*

Nature provides its own color schemes, ready-made sources in a sense, through varying seasons. All can be a constant source of inspiration for successful color mixes—spring greens and yellows, autumnal earth tones and winter whites are just a few of the most obvious ones. Each color mix produces its own very special mood, from cool and fresh to sunny and warm. If you borrow from nature's colors to build a scheme for a room be sure the colors will create the effect you want. The easiest schemes to build are those formed of no more than two colors, so stay with this formula if you lack experience handling color. (See photographs on the next two pages.)

A fresh spring mood is evoked in this charming one-room apartment designed by Shirley Regendahl. She borrowed some of nature's colors for the easy-to-build, two-color scheme. These are chiefly bright yellow, evocative of the first daffodils, and sharp green that brings to mind the first grass after winter. For a sunny mood Shirley splashed bright yellow onto all the walls and the window area, balancing this with a white vinyl floor sparked with a sharp green carpet made into a large-sized area rug. For total coordination throughout the room the designer used a yellow, green and white striped fabric on the sofa-sleeper, window seat and skirted table. Solid yellow and green fabrics are used for the cushions on the various chairs. Small pillows in bright clear tones add just the right accents. The designer selected this green and yellow scheme because she felt it lived well with the Early American reproduction furniture, bringing out their wood tones to advantage. Colorful accessories and lots of plants help to promote the spring-like feeling in the room.

All the burnished colors of autumn come into play in this comfortable den designed by Joan Blutter. The designer began the scheme with the basic shell composed of walls and floor, utilizing a carpet in rich orange, the color of fall leaves, and a wall covering in a soft muted tan. These two colors, plus golds and terra cottas, come together in the fabric used at the windows and for the sofa. This is a stylized pattern reminiscent of the Thirties, which the designer selected for the change of pace it introduced into the basic muted shell. For the same reason she selected a striped velvet for the chairs, which adds extra design interest yet harmonizes with the sofa. This too features all the rich colors of autumn. White accents in the lamp and paintings pick up the white stripe from the chair fabric and highlight the burnished color scheme. When utilizing a monochromatic scheme of this type, the designer suggests using a play of patterns and one strong accent color to introduce needed visual interest. Since this autumnal color scheme is essentially warm, it is best to utilize it in a room that gets cool northern or eastern light, or in one of huge proportions which needs more intimacy.

The whites and browns of a winter landscape come to mind in this sleek multi-purpose room designed as a study and guest room. The springboard for the color scheme was the unusual shag carpeting in brown and black laced with white, reminiscent of frosty ground. The simple yet effective scheme was easy to build from this ready-made source. Brown with an amber-like tone went up onto the walls, while white was splashed over the ceiling, upholstered furniture and certain wood pieces. Black and dark brown show up in accessories, cushions and the painting, and the whole comes together as a rich setting for working or relaxation. This color scheme needs plenty of natural and artificial illumination to make it live successfully and it is ideal to use in a room which gets cold light, since it is basically warm.

EASY WAYS TO BUILD COLOR SCHEMES

There are many ways to build successful color schemes, but if you are inexperienced at handling color it is wise to utilize an easy method. In this way you will make your job much simpler and avoid making those mistakes which cost money.

Three of the most basic and successful ways are known as monochromatic, related and complementary color schemes. These also happen to be the most commonly used.

MONOCHROMATIC   This scheme is developed from one color, used in varying degrees of value and intensity. Several gradations of this one color are repeated throughout a room to create an overall effect of harmony. Apart from introducing a restful background, this type of scheme also takes colorful accessories well, and makes a smooth shell for furniture. Here is an example: If you build your monochromatic scheme around blue, you would use tones that range from the darkest royal blue to the palest sky blue. These tones in all their various gradations and intensities would appear in floor and wall coverings, fabrics for upholstery and draperies. Accent colors superimposed onto this mélange of blues should add a degree of warmth, as blue is a cold color. Good accents are red, yellow, coral and shrimp, apricot, apple green, gold, and always touches of white.

RELATED   This color scheme is created from those hues which are close to each other on the color wheel, and which have a common color denominator. For example, you could begin a related scheme with yellow, then add yellow green or yellow orange. As an alternative you could go in the opposite direction and start at another point of the color wheel. Then you would begin with green blue and add yellow; or yellow, adding orange and red. In general, a related scheme is refreshing, and it gains in decorative interest when the colors have varied intensities and values. Black and white are good accent colors to use with a related scheme, as they bring out the true quality of the other colors.

(See photographs on the next two pages.)

FORMULA: *Natural Color Schemes Inspired by Wood Tones*

Wood is a color even though you may not think of it as such. In fact, many interesting and effective color schemes can be built from the various colors of different woods. They are easy schemes to create, since you are using another type of ready-made source and generally working within one color family, for a monochromatic effect. The lighter-toned woods are the best to use, as darker types tend to create a heavy, even overpowering, look. Depending on the strength of the wood tone used as a color inspiration, you can utilize these schemes in almost any sized room, with any light exposure. Preferably stick to light woods in rooms with warm light, darker tones in rooms that get cool light.

The soft champagne/pecan tones of this plywood paneling are the catalyst for the overall color mood in this tranquil room. Designer Abbey Darer began her scheme with the paneling, installing it in a chevron design for an interesting visual effect more eye-catching than the usual paneled look. She then utilized various gradations of this pale wood tone throughout the room, creating a monochromatic scheme. The sofa was covered with a champagne-and-coffee-colored fabric in a basket-weave pattern, while a light coffee-colored carpet was run wall-to-wall. Both the sofa and the carpet introduce pattern and textural interest necessary in a monochromatic scheme. The painting, blue cushion and blue accessories introduce just the right touch of strong accent color. This wood tone is perfect to use in a small or dark room which needs its dimensions expanded by visual illusion.

This warm traditional room with Early American overtones draws its color mood from the light, almost golden tones of the plywood paneling used for the built-in unit, the window lambrequin and the dados around the room. The handsome reproduction dining table and chairs introduce slightly darker wood tones, but the look is effective. The brown and white patterned wall covering, actually another paneling, and the brown and white gingham blend easily together and with the wood tones. The charming hooked rug pulls all of these brown and wheat shades together underfoot. The white floor and the white-painted molding are smart, sharp accents which highlight the wood tones. This color scheme, built from the rich wood tones of the paneling, introduces much-needed warmth in a cool room; it also helps to dispense with barnlike overtones in an overly large room.

The light, airy overtones of this summer garden room were created through the use of a soft, pale color scheme borrowed from natural wicker, unfinished wood and sisal matting. The designer began the scheme by taking the sisal matting across the floor and up onto the walls and ceiling. The walls and ceiling were given extra architectural interest through the use of beams in unfinished wood, which run vertically and horizontally. The light, natural-colored shell was then ready for the wicker furniture—some of it in the same natural color as the walls, other pieces painted pristine white for cool contrast. The seating pieces were upholstered in brown and white floral and plaid fabrics, for pattern play and extra visual interest. Lots of green plants, both hanging and on the floor, were used to introduce lively but natural color accents which do not spoil the mood of the muted room. This color formula works well in small or dark rooms, since it is so airy and light.

COMPLEMENTARY This scheme is produced through the use of opposites on the color wheel, such as green and red or blue and red. However, these colors are strongly contrasting, lively and vibrant and they need careful distribution within a room. In a complementary scheme it is usually advisable to let one color dominate, with the second color used for small areas of sharp contrast. In this type of scheme you are utilizing a pair of opposites and so you are introducing both warm and cool colors into the room. When the distribution of the two is well done you create a lovely backdrop for furnishings. White is always a good accent color to use with a complementary scheme, and you can also highlight with a combination of black and white.

A READY-MADE SOURCE Another easy formula for building a color scheme is to use a ready-made source, such as a fabric, or a wall or floor covering. All of these products have been designed by color experts, so that in effect you have an easy-to-follow color chart at your finger tips.

A ready-made source also prevents you from making mistakes, as you will be using a combination of colors which have been well mixed for compatibility. To build a color scheme in this way, you simply select one color from the ready-made source and use this as your basic anchor color throughout the room. Second and third colors from the ready-made source are then utilized to balance this and add the necessary accents and highlights.

Other tried and tested formulas which are easy to handle are shown in the picture stories in this chapter and perhaps they will inspire you to breathe new life into a room with color.

6 · How to Give a Room Focus

A room will fail decoratively if it does not have focus. This even includes a seemingly beautiful room that is relatively comfortable and has good looking furniture in it, for without focus any room lacks direction and definition.

Two elements are of primary importance in giving a room focus. These are a focal point and good furniture arrangements. Together they introduce a basic pattern into the room, give it total cohesion and an attractive appearance, so that it functions properly to serve all your living needs.

If you have already decorated a room but find that it is lacking in this necessary direction and cohesion, you can easily correct this without spending any more money or, at worst, for very little outlay.

Your first task is obviously to discover *why* the room is failing. To do this, stand in the middle of the room and view it from all angles. In this way you will be able to ascertain the amount of available space, the overall proportions, and most importantly, all the other elements in it.

Have a notebook handy to jot down your findings and try to be as dispassionate as possible, even ruthless, as you examine every detail, bearing in mind that changes *must* be made to ensure the room's final success. We all own furnishings we are inordinately fond of, but make up your mind to get rid of these pieces if they are detracting from the success of the room.

Let your eyes wander freely around the room to see, first of all, if they are automatically drawn to a focal point. In this way you will quickly be able to divine one of three things: that there is no focal point; that it is too weak to hold your attention; or that the focal point is good but that something else is amiss.

When the focal point is weak or if one does not exist, make a note to correct this error. If something else is making the room lack cohesion, attempt to analyze what this actually is. It could be one of two things. The furniture arrangement or arrangements may be inappropriate for the room, or the furniture may be the wrong scale both for the actual groupings and the room itself.

167

Many rooms are thrown off balance because the furniture has been poorly grouped for the size, shape and function of the room. Sometimes a grouping is haphazard, straggling off in all directions to create an untidy look. Often furniture arrangements are too tightly woven together, so that there is lots of lost space around them. Occasionally there are too many furniture arrangements to allow individual pieces to be seen to advantage, and this also introduces a cluttered, crowded effect. Conversely, there may be too few furniture arrangements and this makes the room appear empty and desolate.

As you analyze the room, you may discover that the focal point is excellent, the furniture properly arranged but that the grouping is slightly defective because the furniture is not of the right scale. The scale of each piece of furniture needs to be properly balanced to its neighbor and to the overall proportions of the room, for a harmonious look.

Once you have ascertained the basic problems in the room, you can go about correcting the mistakes. The simplest way is to make a floor plan of the actual room, measuring the length, width and height in feet. Use a metal coil-spring tape measure as this prevents mistakes. Translate these measurements onto paper, using the scale of one foot equals one inch or half an inch, whichever you find the easiest to work with. Draw in windows and any other architectural elements, so that you can easily view all the important features as well as the basic shape of the room. If you already have a good focal point in the room, be sure to mark this on the plan as this is a major key to revamping the room correctly, for the best effect.

Measure all of your furniture and then rearrange this on paper, penciling in the shapes and forming new groupings, until you find the ones which are the most balanced and attractive for the room. Rearranging the furniture on paper is much simpler and less trying than doing it physically and you are also able to quickly visualize the effects the furniture would create. You will be able to instantly spot furniture that is out of scale in a given arrangement, and pieces which might need to be discarded to give the arrangement more cohesion. You might even find you have to add new pieces to give the grouping a finished appearance. You will also know what you must do about that very necessary focal point.

If there is no focal point, select a wall or an area of the room which is the most suitable for the creation of one. When you have a focal point that is weak and ineffectual, decide how you can revamp it, to give it more visual impact.

When you are decorating from scratch your task is in some ways much simpler, because you have no mistakes to correct. Follow the guidelines just given, make a floor plan and create a center of interest, as well as good furniture arrangements composed of properly scaled pieces. Incidentally, a paper floor plan of this kind is an excellent blueprint in helping you to determine how much furniture you can include for comfort, plus the right shapes and scale to utilize. It also comes in handy as a buying guide, pinpointing the necessary items; it prevents your wasting money on pieces you can't really use or which are too small or too large.

Since focal points and furniture arrangements are the vital elements in creating a successful room, let's look at them more closely.

PROBLEM: *A long, narrow room with a poor window which was unsuitable as a natural focal point; need for a decorative center of interest.*

SOLUTION: *Use of a large antique cabinet, clever grouping of art works and skillful placement of furniture.*

Although a window is an architectural element that can often be turned into a natural focal point, this one was too unattractive to use as such. It also faced onto a poor view.

The owners of this apartment knew that their best solution was to create a new focal point in the room, preferably one on either of the two long walls. They enlisted the aid of interior designer Ving Smith, who set about giving the room a necessary center of gravity. His technique: use of a large antique cabinet, clever grouping of interesting art and skillful placement of furniture to underscore the effect created by the cabinet and art. The antique cabinet, which the owners had formerly used in a large entrance hall of their old apartment, was first revamped. The designer had the inside painted deep red and fitted out with strip lighting. New glass shelves were added and the exterior wood was refinished so that its fine patina showed to advantage. The cabinet was then placed in the center of the long wall on the right side of the room and flanked by groupings of art works on either side. Ving Smith took these from the floor to the ceiling, not only to give the cabinet proper balance but also to introduce strong decorative impact. He used a diverse mixture of items for design and color interest, combining prints, posters, oils, water colors and sketches of various sizes and in all manner of frames, again for visual interest. Pieces of old porcelain and ornaments stand out well against the red interior of the cabinet and the whole wall comes alive with different colors and textures. Once this focal point had been created, the furniture seemed to fall into place almost naturally. The two white

sofas take the center of the floor facing each other across an unusual coffee table made of copper. Ving Smith balanced this furniture arrangement with a fourth piece, the Parsons table placed behind one of the sofas and holding a lamp and accessories. By day draperies are tied back.

OPPOSITE

PROBLEM: A large high-ceilinged room with a small fireplace which was out of proportion for the dimensions; need for a new stronger area of visual interest.

SOLUTION: Paneling carried onto the wall surrounding sliding doors plus shelves for books and displaying accessories.

A fireplace is a natural focal point in a room but sometimes it fails as this, if it is too small or insignificant. That was the basic problem in this large, high-ceilinged room. The fireplace had no impact and the room needed a strong center of interest to introduce decorative definition. The owner created this on

170

the wall surrounding sliding doors leading to the bedroom. Walnut paneling, which already existed on the back wall, was repeated around the doors and then particleboard shelves were installed over the paneling. These shelves, running floor to ceiling, were used to house books and display accessories. This treatment immediately created that necessary center of visual interest. With this wall completed, the owner arranged the furniture accordingly. The fireplace was simply painted white and the wall above given a dominant painting; the sofa and chairs plus a coffee table were grouped in front of the fireplace. This room proves the point that a center of eye interest does not always have to be the crux of a furniture arrangement. Sometimes it can be an attractive backdrop to a grouping, providing it produces the necessary visual impact and decorative definition in a room.

PROBLEM: *A second bedroom with no space in which to create a focal point or group furniture effectively.*

SOLUTION: *An interesting window treatment for the focal point, plus a simple yet effective furniture arrangement.*

This second bedroom in a city apartment was so small its owner at first thought there was no way to decorate it well and saw it only as a possible catch-all for junk and luggage. Since space was at a premium she decided to ask the advice of an interior designer, who helped her transform it into livable quarters.

All very tiny rooms are hard to decorate and this one was no exception. Its confined dimensions virtually precluded the use of anything other than a bed and there was no obvious spot to create that necessary center of interest. One of the obstacles in the room was the oddly positioned window with its protruding side and ceiling beams. However, the designer saw this window as a possibility for the center of interest in the room. She began by painting the room a vivid yellow to create a sunny effect and then she added a plywood lambrequin to the window wall. In her search for a drapery fabric she found a summer-fresh floral in just the right yellow, which had a wide border of double trellis. She cleverly utilized this border for the lambrequin, cutting it from the fabric and attaching it to the lambrequin with special adhesive. The lambrequin not only camouflages the protruding beams but acts as a definitive frame for the draperies. Each drapery was treated differently, one left hanging loose, the other tied back for an interesting change of pace and to disguise the awkward placement of the window. Extra pieces of the fabric's border were utilized for the dust ruffle on the bed; other left-over pieces of fabric became upholstery on the small headboard made of plywood covered with foam rubber. A lightly quilted cotton spread in the same yellow as the walls adds color coordination in the room, as does a collection of small pillows. A yellow Flokati rug was added for warmth underfoot. To conserve space, the bed was placed close to the window, leaving enough room for the antique chest which holds the lamp. A room that was once an eyesore and hard to bring into line gains comfort and decorative good looks, with the window treatment acting as the center of eye interest, underscored by the placement of the dressed-up bed.

THE IMPORTANCE OF A FOCAL POINT

Every room in your home, with the exception of kitchen and bathroom, requires a focal point. A focal point is the center of interest around which all other elements revolve; it therefore helps to give a room a meaningful pattern. Because the eye is automatically drawn to it, a focal point should have strong visual interest and attractiveness.

Certain rooms have ready-made focal points, such as a fireplace or handsome windows. These can be skillfully decorated so that they become the most dominant point of interest in the room, the anchor for a decorative scheme. But not all rooms have these natural focal points and it is usually necessary to create your own. There are many good ideas that can be successfully adopted and they are relatively simple to do yourself. Most of them are inexpensive, not an unimportant consideration when you are working on a small budget. Each one helps to give a room that all-important starting point, so that you can then plan furniture arrangements for the ultimate in appearance and comfort. Actually, once the focal point is in place you will find that furniture groupings quickly clarify themselves, almost falling into position naturally. Together they give a room cohesion and add that much needed focus of attention.

If you are lucky enough to have a natural focal point in a room, it is wise to take advantage of it. If you do not have an obvious center of interest, such as good windows or a fireplace, then you must choose an area that can be given one. Generally, the largest wall in a room is the most appropriate spot for introducing a center of visual interest.

It is important to remember that the size of a focal point should be scaled in correct proportion to the dimensions of the room. For instance, a large room obviously needs a very dominant focal point that has its own built-in strength, one which does not look insignificant for the size of the room. On the other hand, a small room needs a center of interest that is smaller and more balanced in proportion to the diminutive dimensions.

Incidentally, I think it is worth pointing out here that although a focal point is called *a center of interest* it does not necessarily have to be actually in the *center* of the room. It can be almost anywhere, but it *must* be the pivot around which all other furnishings flow. There should always be one focal point in a room, whatever its size and shape. In a spacious room you can also add a secondary, smaller center of interest, providing the two do not fight each other.

Think of a focal point as a directional arrow which clearly indicates the proper pattern for all other furnishings within the room, for the best appearance and function.

PROBLEM: A small living room which failed because it had no real center of decorative interest.

SOLUTION: A paneled wall-hung furniture system and skillful use of accessories.

Most rooms, especially small ones, fail if they are without a focal point. But the problem was more than adequately solved here through the use of a wall-hung furniture system. A short blank wall was instantly transformed in importance through the addition of Bangkok teak paneling and matching wall-hung pieces of furniture. It makes a compact area housing entertainment equipment of all kinds, as well as books and decorative acessories. The latter help to give the wall strong visual interest and turn it into a focal point. The secret was in the mingling of diverse items: sculpture, prints, an old map, fruit and flowers along with the books. The beauty of this type of system is that it takes up no floor space, unlike a dominant piece of furniture used to create a striking center of gravity.

PROBLEM: Old-fashioned room with very little furniture, no strong architectural features; need for a focal point to dispense with unfurnished look and to pull the room together.

SOLUTION: Ingenious wall and floor treatments coordinated in design, color and texture to create focus; rearrangement of furniture to its best advantage and to underscore these features.

This bedroom was badly furnished and had a bedraggled look. Its owner, a young career girl, wanted to give it new life, decorative focus and make it function as a den as well.

The occupant of this old-fashioned city apartment faced serious problems with the decoration of the bedroom. Apart from its very unattractive overtones, and architectural oddities such as the numerous protruding beams, it lacked decorative cohesion. This sprang from its shortage of furniture and color. The owner enlisted the help of interior designer Virginia Frankel, who redecorated the room with skill and imagination rather than a large expenditure of money. In fact, the room was done on a budget. The designer first painted the walls and ceiling white to introduce light, airy overtones. She then put down green cushioned-vinyl flooring in the center of the room, bordering this with the same type of vinyl in white and then green again, for a custom-designed look underfoot. To create a center of eye interest in the room, Virginia created a supergraphics effect on the long back wall, utilizing a panel and an arc of the same green floor covering. These were carefully positioned to follow the design of the floor. To unify the two windows and camouflage the protruding beams, the designer covered the entire window wall with woven blinds and added a matching valance. The blinds, striped in pink, red, orange and white, inject the necessary vivid accent color into the green-and-white shell; these colors are repeated throughout for coordination. The furniture was then rearranged more effectively for comfort and good looks. The designer placed the bed along the wall, instead of jutting out, and dressed it up with a red spread, striped across the top with pink and orange to match the colors of the window blinds. A collection of white, red and green pillows adds just the necessary finishing touch, while a poster hung to the left adds balance and further color interest on the back wall. The two wicker baskets the occupant already owned were resprayed spanking white and utilized at each end of the bed for the necessary accessories and telephone. A crimson oval rug placed immediately in front of the bed, which also serves as a sofa, fulfills the color scheme. Since the young owner wanted to include a desk in her bedroom-den but could not afford to buy one, Virginia created a work surface with a wood counter covered in the green vinyl flooring, plus an inexpensive white campaign chest. This was placed under the windows and topped with the counter, which was secured to the wall. An old wicker stool was revamped with white paint to service the dressing-table end of the counter, while an inexpensive director's chair was purchased to serve the desk portion. Inexpensive accessories and plants were used to add that final fillip to the redecorated room, which gains a whole new look through the clever focal point and interesting rearrangement of the furniture.

IDEAS FOR FOCAL POINTS

After you have selected the spot where you want to create your focal point, your next task is to decide on the kind which is most suitable for the room. Two things are of prime importance: the focal point should blend well with the style of furniture you intend to use and it should not be too expensive for your budget. Here are some ideas which might offer you inspiration and also help you to give a room focus.

THE FIREPLACE As I pointed out earlier, a fireplace is the most traditional of all focal points; if you are lucky enough to have one, play it up to the fullest. The important thing to remember is that a fireplace, whatever its style or size, simply cannot stand alone as a center of interest. The wall in which it is set must also have visual impact, so that together the two give the room focus.

The actual style of the fireplace will help you to determine the best treatment for the wall. Obviously a traditional fireplace needs to be properly balanced with traditional accessories; a modern fireplace with more contemporary items. It is also a good idea to paint the wall a contrasting color or give it a wall covering, so that the mantleshelf and fireplace surround stand out effectively. If the wood of a fireplace surround is damaged or old, you can create handsome new looks through the use of spray-on lacquer or paint.

A traditional fireplace in a traditional room should be treated in an appropriate style. In other words, the wall above should be decorated with a mirror or a painting, flanked on either side by wall sconces if space permits. If the fireplace is set on a long wall, use supplementary groupings of art on either side of the fireplace area to add necessary balance.

A modern fireplace also lends itself to a variety of eye-catching treatments. Once again, the area of wall immediately above the fireplace should be given a mirror or a painting, or alternatively an interesting piece of sculpture which can easily be hung or a construction painting, to add definition. The flanking wall areas can be enhanced with groupings of art, prints and posters, these in turn perhaps balanced by plants or a pedestal holding a piece of sculpture. If a modern fireplace has a long hearth it can be turned into an attractive seating area through the addition of cushions. Or it might be enlivened with a collection of plants, old baskets, copper and brass items or again a piece of interesting sculpture.

Both traditional and modern fireplaces can be given extra focus through the addition of floor-to-ceiling bookshelves on either side. When the books are interspersed with an array of colorful accessories, art work and plants the whole area gains in dramatic visual impact.

If a fireplace appeals to you in a room without one, there are a variety of ways to include one. For instance, you can use a free-standing porcelain stove in a room with a traditional flavor; alternatively you might choose a more modern free-standing stove in a room which has contemporary overtones. You can also create a fireplace facade, through the addition of a mantleshelf and a hearth made of wood, metal-covered wood, brick or slate. Once the shelf and hearth have been attached to the walls, these can be decorated with various items. The hearth itself can be dressed up with andirons and logs or an electric fire that simulates burning logs. Even one of the free-standing stoves just mentioned works on a hearth. The mantle can be highlighted with all manner of accessories.

If you prefer, actual mantles and surrounds, usually of period design, can be found in second-hand stores and junk shops, and these can be utilized in the same manner. Naturally, these usually require a little repolishing or refinishing with paint, and they stand out best when highlighted with traditional accessories.

A fireplace is a good central pivot for any seating arrangement, since it acts as the perfect arrow showing you exactly where to place the furniture for the most handsome effects.

WINDOWS   Good windows are also a natural focal point in a room, and they can be treated in many ways to become the center of visual interest. The kind of treatment you select depends, of course, on the style and size of the window and, most importantly, the view.

Windows that face onto a spectacular vista, such as the sea, the mountains, a country landscape or a rooftop cityscape obviously have great assets. The view itself can be turned into a special feature; in fact, it can often be a breathtaking focal point.

When you have windows with this type of view, it is best to underplay the window treatment. Choose simple curtains to form a soft frame or leave the glass itself bare. As an alternative, you can use a wooden lambrequin covered with a fabric or wall covering, or a window-length valance and simple side draperies tied back. Again, these subtly frame the window and permit the view to be properly seen. Any kind of elaborate treatment will detract from the view and so weaken the window as a strong focal point.

If you have good or unusual windows which happen to face an ugly or uninteresting view, these can be given an imaginative treatment which will make them the center of interest in the room. The treatment must have lots of design interest and it should extend onto the adjoining walls at each side of the window, so that the eye is pulled towards the entire wall. It should also be the type of treatment that stops the eye at the window and does not lead it out. This type of dramatic window treatment along a whole wall makes a superb backdrop for a well-planned furniture arrangement. The mediocre view can be camouflaged by curtains, blinds, window shades, sheer draperies, vertical blinds, shelves of plants or combinations of these elements. It is possible to be much more elaborate with this type of window, since you are mainly creating interest within the room and not drawing attention to the outside view.

Bay and bow windows also offer lots of possibilities as focal points. The intrinsic shape of this type of window makes it ideal for a small furniture arrangement or a dramatic piece of furniture, such as a porcelain stove, an antique chest or a small etagere. The furniture used should be backed up by a clever window treatment, preferably one that acts as a backdrop. In combination the two increase the window's gravitational pull as a striking focal point.

WALL TREATMENTS   Almost any wall in a room can be turned into an interesting focal point, through the use of a variety of products. You can select from furniture to wall coverings, shelves of books to groupings of art.

You can achieve dramatic effects by using floor-to-ceiling shelves filled with books. Book jackets in themselves are very colorful and can be arranged to produce vivid areas of concentrated color on the shelves. An even stronger visual effect is created when decorative objects are scattered among the books, such as ornaments, shells, mineral rocks, plants, flowers and paintings or photographs.

When interior designer John Elmo utilizes a wall of books to create a focal point in a room, he always keeps a central area of the lower wall space free, for a desk, a writing table or sofa. He likes to build this kind of wallscape, as he believes it introduces a visual change of pace along the wall and so adds extra design interest.

This same designer often creates a focal point through the use of mirror. He will cover the wall with plain or smoked mirror, running it the length of the wall and taking it from the floor to the ceiling. He then decorates this wall of mirror with decorative objects, perhaps an antique mirror hung upon the mirrored wall or an interesting painting. He then flanks the mirror painting with wall sconces. Next, he creates a furniture grouping in front of the mirrored and decorated wall. John particularly likes this idea for small dining rooms, or small living rooms, since it also helps to expand space at the same time.

A mural or a panel of scenic wallpaper will bring a bare wall into focus, and this is extremely inexpensive to do. An interesting garden scene, or any other outdoor scene, cleverly draws the eye out and beyond, for an almost three-dimensional effect. It makes an excellent center of visual interest because it gives the room a "view." It works well in any small room since it helps to expand the dimensions of the area by illusion but does not intrude on floor space.

A wall grouping of paintings, posters, prints, mirrors, needlepoint pictures and wooden plaques can be skillfully arranged on a wall to introduce a play of color, texture and design. This is one of the most popular ways to give a room focus, especially when the grouping is backed up by a good furniture arrangement. Art works displayed in this manner can be related in theme and color or totally different. It's always a good idea to use various sizes and shapes and different frames, so that you introduce a feeling of movement. The secret of their eye appeal is in their variation.

PROBLEM: A one-room apartment which had to work around the clock and required furniture to service all living needs.

SOLUTION: Use of carefully selected, well-scaled furniture in comfortable and attractive groupings for the best in function and appearance.

The living-sleeping area of this one-room apartment was short on space, drab and dreary in appearance. It is seen here from the kitchen through the kitchen passway.

PHOTO ON FOLLOWING PAGE

Once the all-purpose room of this one-room apartment had been enlivened with a cheerful sunny yellow and white scheme, the well-chosen furniture, selected for its scale and good looks, was positioned. The idea was to create an airy open arrangement for the best in function and looks. Since the seating-sleeping area was the most important, this was arranged first. The yellow sleep sofa was positioned against the main wall, backed up by a Parsons-table desk to one side, used instead of a small end table. The thought here was to conserve

space as much as possible and the desk was the perfect solution. It provides necessary working surface and also doubles as an end table, while adding balance to the arrangement. A small chair and a stool both push under the desk, yet can be brought out to partner the sofa when extra seating is required. An English antique chair and a small French antique table were positioned opposite the sofa at an angle, but these pieces are linked to the major seating piece through the area rug which pulls them all together visually. Since confined space precluded the use of a dining table, the owner built a buffet server which extends on both sides of the kitchen passway. The buffet seats four people, two on each side of the passway. Tall stools, stored in the kitchen, are brought out for use at the living room side. Well-placed lamps provide good illumination in the room.

OPPOSITE

Here you can see the wall facing the sofa, and the rest of the all-purpose room. The tall cabinet was positioned on this wall to act as a necessary focal point for the room and to add balance. The piece is easily put together by a handyman and is made of perforated hardboard. It hides TV and hi-fi as well as functioning for clothes storage and books. Decorative objects on the center shelves add visual interest. A second English chair, placed in the corner near the window, can also be brought into the main area of the room when required. Lots of plants and a wicker basket fill out odd blank spots in the room.

PROBLEM: A tiny one-room apartment required to double as a studio for a freelance commercial artist.

SOLUTION: Clever alignment of space through skillful furniture arrangement and use of a built-in seating-sleeping unit backed up by good storage piece.

This tiny one-room apartment also had to serve as a studio for the young occupant, a commercial artist. Apart from requiring the normal living conveniences and furniture, she needed a good work surface and plenty of storage facilities for her artist's materials as well as clothes and other items. Peggy Walker provided for all these needs, using the limited area effectively and dramatically for the best in function and appearance. Her technique was clever alignment of furniture and utilization of a unique built-in. The components are actually all free-standing and are simply pushed together to create the long unit shown. These pieces are a wooden storage chest used as a base for the mattress, a tall storage cupboard at one end of the base piece, shelves above the cupboard, and a Parsons table placed at the other end. Drawers under the bed, which acts as a sofa by day, store all manner of clothes and linens, while artist's materials fit neatly into the deep cupboard, which opens at the front. This also provides surface space for a lamp, clock, telephone and accessories. The Parsons table, covered with a hardy plastic laminate, sees triple service as drawing board, desk and dining table. The steel and cane chair is simply pushed underneath the table to conserve space, or it can be brought out to provide extra seating when required. By organizing all these pieces into a few feet of space, the designer left the rest of the room free for other necessary pieces of furniture, such as two comfortable arm chairs, a coffee table and small end tables. More shelves are wall hung to save space and to house books, records, hi-fi–TV and accessories. (This other area of the room is not shown in the picture.) Underscoring the colorful looks of the bedspread, cushions and painting, is the handsome area rug. This is perfectly scaled for the size of the room and the built-in unit, and it acts as a strong visual focal point here. Apart from fulfilling the color scheme it adds textural and design interest on the bare wood floor. This room illustrates how a good furniture arrangement can bring focus and function to a small area of space.

PROBLEM: A brick fireplace wall which needed to be given more visual interest.

SOLUTION: Built-in shelves to one side of the fireplace; use of vivid color; addition of furniture and accessories.

This living room was furnished handsomely yet it lacked decorative impact. The brick fireplace, obviously the natural focal point, was a charming touch in a city apartment and added a degree of character to the room. However it was somewhat dull and uninteresting, flanked on either side by white walls. Interior designer Peggy Walker realized that dressing up the fireplace itself with accessories was simply not enough; the whole wall needed to be brought into focus. She created real visual interest in the area through the use of built-in shelves which she carried from the floor to the ceiling. These were then filled with books and accessories for color and textural play. To enliven the brick fireplace she added a vivid painting framed in red, a red vase and a firescreen slashed with red across the top. To reinforce the touches of red here and on the bookshelves, she grouped some small red pieces of furniture next to the built-in unit. Her selections were a graceful Bertoia chair and ottoman upholstered in red wool and a small red plastic table. The result: a fireplace wall revitalized into a colorful focal point plus a comfortable reading corner.

PROBLEM: *Poorly arranged sectional seating which gave small room a cluttered look; lack of any dominant wood pieces required to add balance.*

SOLUTION: *Regrouping of the sectional seating pieces for an airier look, plus the addition of a rug, bookshelves and plants to balance seating area.*

The newlyweds who own this apartment were unhappy with many elements. They found the white walls and beige carpet installation they had inherited very drab, and so spent most of their budget on the bright rust sectional seating pieces. This left them very little to invest in other extra pieces of furniture, required to add the necessary balance and proportion in the room. They asked interior designer Peggy Walker to revamp the apartment, without spending very much money. The designer began by breaking up the grouping of the sectional pieces, which had been arranged to form two small love seats facing each other, with an ottoman to one side and the circular stack tables in between. She felt this central arrangement was breaking up the space badly. Her solution was to group the sectional seating pieces in an L-shape down the main wall, turning the corner in front of the window. This at once opened up the central floor space. Since the owners could not afford to buy any additional furniture, Peggy had two long shelves built inexpensively and these were hung on the center of the wall, above the sectional seating arrangements. With the addition of a lamp, books, plants and accessories, the shelves introduce needed balance on the wall; underscoring this effect are the two prints, which Peggy moved from the bedroom and hung next to the shelves. One circular stack table was placed at one end of the sectional grouping, and a second one services this area and a small chair (not shown in picture). Since the beige carpet was displeasing to the owners, Peggy covered a portion of this with a brightly colored area rug, which adds visual interest in front of the seating arrangement and pulls all the elements together. To add a touch of needed height, the designer placed a tall tree in front of the window, rounding this out with smaller plants. Some bright cushions and a modern floor lamp complete the revamp, which was done on a minute budget.

PROBLEM: *Large living room with many windows which broke up wall space and made it impossible to arrange furniture effectively.*

SOLUTION: *Furniture arrangements devised to work in the central area of space, backed up by clever placement of small decorative pieces.*

BEFORE

Although this living room of a country house was spacious and airy, its many windows made it difficult to arrange the furniture well. Lack of wall space meant utilizing the central area of space, but the owners were unsure about doing this successfully themselves.

AFTER

The owners enlisted the aid of interior designer Virginia Frankel, who turned the many windows to advantage and created a whole new ambiance through the skillful placement of furniture and accessories. Since the owners wanted to totally redecorate, the designer began by revamping the shell. She removed old heating units under the windows and installed new, less obvious ones; she also added ceiling beams to introduce architectural interest. The walls were painted a soft coffee color and the floor was covered with a vinyl asbestos tile with a wood-grain effect in a parquet pattern. Windows were given more balance through the addition of floor-length draperies in a sheer fabric, hung on white painted rods. With the shell in place, the designer then tackled the arrangement of the furniture. The most important new piece was a long three-seater sofa and Virginia placed this at one end of the room, facing a large window. She then backed this up with a white storage-bookshelf unit, the exact height of the sofa, which acts as a sofa table. The bookshelves face into the room. Her next addition was a love seat matched to the sofa, positioned to form an L-shape effect jutting out from the bookshelf unit, which acts as a divider in the center of the room. Area rugs in tones of coffee and white plus small decorative tables play up each seating area. With this unique, eye-catching central arrangement in position, pieces for the rest of the room seemed to fall naturally into place. Virginia used a number of wicker chairs and ottomans, covered in the sofa fabric, to fill out the two areas of the central seating grouping; tall plants were utilized to decorate blank corners, while more plants were hung from the ceiling and beams. The whole mood is garden-fresh, with the central furniture arrangement providing necessary comfort, function and cohesion in the room.

FURNITURE ARRANGEMENTS

To my mind, focal points and furniture arrangements work together to create that necessary focus in a room. Once you have created your gravitational center of interest, your furniture arrangements will clarify themselves and seem to fall into place automatically.

A furniture arrangement has three essential requirements:
1. It should be attractive.
2. It must have intrinsic comfort.
3. It must suit your living needs to the fullest.

It is important to bear these points in mind as you plan your furniture groupings. As was pointed out earlier, do them on paper first, to avoid making mistakes and wasting time, energy and money. Any room will benefit from this paper tryout, since you can experiment until you find the furniture groupings which please you the most. A good grouping is one which can be viewed from any part of the room without loss of its visual attractiveness. Make sure that the grouping is well defined and uncluttered, and always allow for traffic patterns. This is extremely important, as any furniture arrangement has to function for the human element, those who will occupy the room. It needs to be comfortable for conversing and convenient for movement within the room. People have to enter, cross and leave a room, so always indicate traffic lanes on your floor plans.

The following points will guide you when you plan your furniture arrangements.

• Light-scaled furniture creates an illusion of spaciousness—an important consideration when decorating a small room or creating two furniture arrangements within one room.

• Heavy furniture looks larger than it really is when placed in the center of a room. It is advisable to position bulky pieces against a wall. This saves floor space.

• Group a sofa and chairs or several chairs in a pattern that allows traffic to move around and not through the grouping.

• Two or more large pieces of furniture in one grouping create an unbalanced look. Separate large pieces so that the room does not look too heavy in one area.

• Pieces utilized in a conversation arrangement should be grouped fairly close together, as people dislike shouting across a room.

• Use end tables and lamp tables that are similar in height to the arms of sofas and chairs. This ensures proper balance to the grouping, provides comfort and prevents accidents with drinks.

• Always include end tables or coffee tables in a conversation grouping, for convenient placement of lamps, ashtrays etc.

• Select table or floor lamps that are the correct height when placed ‹t to seating pieces. This ensures adequate illumination and comfort in the area.

• Make sure all the furniture is balanced in height and scale for harmony.

• Do not huddle too many wood pieces with legs close together. This introduces a "forest" look at floor level which is disconcerting.

• When using upholstered pieces always include several wood pieces, to counteract an overstuffed look. These can be end tables, coffee tables or chairs. Steel-and-glass or plexiglass pieces can also be incorporated to introduce a change of visual pace.

When creating a furniture arrangement it is best to start with the strongest or largest piece of furniture. This acts as the core of the furniture pattern, around which the lesser pieces can flow. It also helps to simplify the arranging.

The main furniture grouping in any room must be highly functional, whether this is for seating, dining, entertaining, sleeping or pursuing hobbies. Supplemental or secondary arrangements can be created, to provide for other activities, or they can be purely decorative, placed against a wall.

PHOTO ON FOLLOWING PAGE

The young actress who decorated this apartment for herself started out with only one basic possession, the large, brand-new piece of nylon shag carpet donated by her brother. Although she liked the tweedy mixture of the red, white and blue, she did not want to repeat these colors anywhere else in the room, feeling them to be too strong and overpowering for her tastes and the size of the room. Her preference was for white-on-white, to promote the feeling of a cool oasis in the city and to introduce extra spaciousness. She painted the walls herself, using bright white to push the walls out; white was carried over onto the window in the tie-back draperies which she made herself from an inexpensive fabric. The ugly old-fashioned window was concealed by a net curtain hung close to the glass and falling below the sill. Her major purchase was the white sofa, more practical than it looks as it is covered with vinyl that is hardy and repels staining; it is simple to sponge clean of any surface dirt. The sofa was partnered with two moderately priced director's chairs, again in white to fulfill the color scheme. To add balance to the white pieces an unfinished wood Parsons end table was lacquered black, another do-it-yourself job easily accomplished with several cans of spray-on lac-

quer. Since the small budget precluded the purchase of a coffee table, the young amateur decorator utilized two plexiglass pedestals bought cheaply in a department store sale. The handsome lamp and homemade cushions introduce extra decorative touches, as do the plants which were purchased as her budget permitted. The unusual-looking birdcage was found on a holiday in Venezuela and brought back to add its own special charm to the room. It also promoted the actress to become a bird fancier and her current pets include Siberian goldfinches, a crested Gloucester canary, a Wydah and its mate, all shown in the cage. Incidentally, the easy-care nylon carpeting takes birds and plants in its stride, as any overflow can be cleaned up quickly and easily.

7 · Budget Decorating Ideas

Almost everyone is interested in budget decorating these days, whether it's for a first decorating job starting from scratch or for a revamp of a room already decorated. Budget ideas can be easily utilized for both, carried through one room or a whole home. Certainly there are enough ideas to choose from, for treating walls, floors and windows and furnishing in general.

Everyone has a different understanding of the word *budget*, but what I am going to deal with in this chapter are small budgets and ways to decorate well without spending a great deal of money.

Of course the real secret of budget decorating is not so much the amount of money you spend, but the skillful use of products and ideas which bring flair, good looks and comfort to your home. This is what really counts. Imagination and ingenuity are your best tools for creating sparkling new looks and a pleasant, compatible ambiance for day to day living.

In point of fact, budget decorating has never been easier than it is today. There are all kinds of new products you can utilize, from all the latest spray-on paints and self-adhesive wall coverings to flooring materials you can put down yourself. Budget-priced furniture is readily available and the newest designs are handsome and don't scream "budget" at you. For instance, you can select unfinished wood furniture you paint yourself, plastic and plexiglass pieces as well as chrome-and-glass items which no longer cost the earth. Much of this new furniture features good vinyls that simulate leather and suede upholstery and which also help to lower the cost considerably.

Then again, accessories which add the necessary finishing touch to a room are more plentiful than ever before. Items found in foreign import shops and even dime stores help you to work wonders in a room whilst staying within a limited budget. All of these items, along with plants, cushions, shells, posters and prints, add color and design interest to any room, and when they are handled with flair they dispense with that budget look altogether.

Finally, you have one other important decorating element which has no price tag at all . . . color. As I pointed out in the chapter devoted to color, bright zingy shades cost no more than dull, drab ones. A good color scheme helps to enhance any room enormously and it often dispenses with the need for lots of costly furniture. Color can go on the walls, the floor, the windows and wash over furniture, bringing fresh new overtones to the most inexpensively furnished room. Don't neglect it, but instead use it to create a mood, hide architectural faults or highlight special features.

Three elements come together in a room to create the overall background—the shell for furniture, furnishings and accessories. These are the walls, the floor and the windows. Let us take a look at some budget ideas for all of these elements, before considering budget-minded furniture and accessories.

The latest put-together furniture was utilized in this budget-wise living room by designer Peggy Walker. All of the seating pieces and tables in the room are composed of good looking tubular sections, plus tops, which fit together with easy precision and come in small boxes. In fact the entire conversation grouping in this room was carried home by hand and assembled in no time at all. They are also inexpensive and thus ideal for a budget scheme. The designer selected white, with yellow upholstery, to introduce verve into the basically traditional shell and to contrast with the bright blue carpet. The window wall has been handled with great decorative vitality and also at small cost. Inexpensive grass green and white striped window shades were reversed on their rollers and hung within the handsome old frames to echo the broader stripes around them. The designer added stick-on tape in blue and yellow across their borders for a custom touch, along with white ring pulls. Home carpentry produced the "built-outs" below that add extra shelf space to accommodate a small TV set and knickknacks. These open-end boxes sit snugly over the sills and house a second set of shades; one to conceal extra storage and the other to act as a pull-down over the radiator. This whole series of colorful surprises, stirred into the stimulating pattern mix, creates a serene environment that is as easy to live with as it was to purchase.

BUDGET-WISE FLOORS

I am starting with the floor because this is usually considered the most expensive to treat effectively, probably because you have the cost of a floor covering plus the price of installing it.

You may dream of lush wall-to-wall broadloom carpeting, a fine Oriental or Persian area rug, or a sparkling marble floor. But if the budget doesn't permit you to buy any of these, you will have to "make do" with what you can afford.

Today "making do" is not as terrible as it sounds, thanks to all the latest budget floor coverings. You may not be able to afford expensive wool broadloom carpeting, but this does not mean that you cannot have this particular look in a room if you wish. Manufacturers are currently producing very good broadloom carpeting made of such fibers as nylon, polyester, acrylic and olefin. All of these have the look of wool and the colors are very varied, ranging from pastels to vivid hot colors. All of these man-made-fiber carpets are cheaper than wool, yet they create the same effect underfoot. I happen to consider them extremely budget-minded since they are very durable and long lasting, easy to spot-clean with soap-and-water sponging and some of them even have soil-hiding properties.

So, if that smooth, flowing carpeted effect is your preference look at some of these carpets now on the market. A word of advice: Always check the manufacturer's name and select the better known name brands, so that you are assured of getting a good product. Look for those carpets bearing the manufacturer's five-year wearing guarantee, as they are excellent buys.

Any type of wall-to-wall carpeting should be put down over an underlay or padding, to prolong its life span. You will therefore still have the cost of this, plus the price of the installation. However, since you are saving on the actual purchase price of the carpet, by choosing a man-made fiber instead of wool, you will inevitably save a considerable amount of money. With a little thought and careful shopping around, you will discover that you can carpet a room for much less than you thought at first. On a budget, in fact.

If you find the price of synthetic carpeting still too prohibitive for your budget, yet wish to have a carpeted effect, you should consider carpet tiles. These are a fairly new product on the market and are mostly made of hard-wearing nylon. They have an extremely good appearance and are available in a variety of patterns and colors. It is easy to simulate the look of wall-to-wall carpeting by utilizing these tiles throughout a room. You can introduce a one-color effect or pattern, by using tiles of one color or intermingling different colors.

Carpet tiles are much cheaper than broadloom carpet and most of them come with a foam rubber backing, which immediately dispenses with the need for underlay. Since they also have a self-adhering backing, you will find them easy to put down yourself. In this way you dispense with the price of the underlay and the cost of installation.

If you don't particularly want a carpeted look, there are a variety of other ways to treat a floor on a small budget. However, before you even consider another type of product it is advisable to examine the actual floor of the room to be decorated. You may find that it is made of a good wood, which can be repolished or refinished. Dark stains are available at most paint shops and these are easy to use yourself. Once the floor has been stained, it can be polished or treated to several coats of polyurethane varnish, to give it a high gloss. This latter treatment also dispenses with the need for continual waxing.

If you want to do something a little more interesting with a wood floor, you might consider painting it a light color, such as white or cream. This is a popular idea with interior designers at the moment. Once the floor has been given several coats of the light paint it is allowed to dry and then coated with several layers of polyurethane varnish. This seals in the paint and protects it from scuffing and marking.

Anyone who is clever with a paintbrush and artistically minded can decorate a painted floor with a stenciled pattern for added interest. This might be an all-over pattern composed of a single flower carried across the floor in horizontal or vertical lines, or it could be a random design. A simple border of geometric designs or flowers is also eye-catching and easy to do yourself. The floor should be sealed with the polyurethane varnish after the pattern has dried, again for protection and long wearability.

All kinds of area rugs add decorative interest to polished or painted wood floors. Today you have a wide range of budget-minded buys, from the modern Danish ryas to clever copies of Orientals and Persians. Flokati rugs from Greece and interesting woven patterns from Spain and Morocco are also moderately priced and they introduce color, pattern and texture to any smooth floor.

Another way to treat a floor in a budget-minded room is to cover it

197

with fabric. This introduces a very novel effect that is most attractive, especially in bedrooms or dining rooms which take less traffic. The fabric is stretched tightly across the floor, wall-to-wall, and then attached with special adhesive. Once it is in place and after the adhesive has dried, the fabric is coated with half a dozen coats of clear polyurethane varnish. This seals and protects it. Custom-designed looks can be introduced if you carry the same fabric throughout the room, on the walls and for draperies or for upholstered pieces.

All vinyls, both tiles and sheets, are budget-minded flooring products. There is an enormous selection of colors, patterns and designs available today from a host of good manufacturers and interesting effects can be created at low cost. Vinyl asbestos tiles are about the cheapest available and, apart from being hard-wearing, they are now being made in an extensive range of colors and patterns. These and other vinyl tiles enable you to create custom-designed effects through various combinations, and with a little imagination and ingenuity you achieve striking results. Vinyls are now being manufactured to simulate brick, tiles, wood, marble, leather, and ceramic tiles, so that your possibilities for a handsome but inexpensive floor are unlimited.

BUDGET-MINDED WALLS

To my mind the best way to decorate walls on a budget is to use paint. It is actually the most inexpensive product available and of course the easiest to handle yourself. Good paints come in all the colors of the rainbow today—you can wash the walls with sunny yellow, cool green

Budget-wise furniture is better made and more attractive than it ever was, and it was used in this apartment along with built-ins and colorful fabrics. The decorating scheme began with the shell of the room. The walls were painted a bright sunny yellow, balanced by a white vinyl floor covering for a light look underfoot. A comfortable and roomy built-in unit was added to the window wall, to provide plenty of seating. The plywood base was painted yellow to match the walls and finished with upholstered seats and back pads covered in cheery red, yellow and orange striped fabric. This same fabric reappears in the Roman shades at the windows and on the pull-up ottomans. The dining and bar coordinates include the game-dining table, chairs, bar and bar chairs. The attractive table extends when required and is made of chrome with a plastic laminated top which simulates butcher block. Chrome chairs have red and yellow upholstery, as do the taller matching bar chairs. The bar itself is made of white melamine with a smoked acrylic front panel. Inexpensive shelves wall-hung behind the bar are practical and handy for bar utensils and glasses. The small square of red nylon carpet adds extra color on the floor and, along with the low-priced cube table, adds definition to the seating area.

or white, hot apricot and shrimp or tranquil sky blue. There is no color limit any more, and color does help to introduce a more furnished look into any room.

If you prefer to introduce pattern as well as color onto your walls, you can choose from a good range of medium- and low-priced wall coverings today. If you are on a very tight budget, it is a good idea to seek out those wall coverings which come pre-trimmed and pre-pasted, which are simple to put up yourself. The pre-pasted wall coverings are brushed with water and then placed on the wall. Some of them are strippable, which means you can quickly pull them off if you have made an error or mismatched a pattern.

Walls that are badly marked or cracked can be covered with most wallpapers and vinyl-type wall coverings; fabric is another way to camouflage marred walls. If you prefer to utilize fabric, select one of medium weight and attach it with either an adhesive or staples. There are a variety of inexpensive fabrics suitable for use on the walls. Sheets also make an ideal wall covering and patterns are prettier than ever today. You can create a lovely custom look in a room by covering the walls with sheets, using them for draperies and upholstery as well as on the bed. Sheets can be attached to the walls with a staple gun or tacked into position. This latter methods means they can be easily removed for laundering when they are soiled.

OPPOSITE BOTTOM

This nursery was decorated on a limited budget by interior designer Virginia Frankel. Its chief ingredients were a colorful vinyl wallpaper, an unfinished wood cupboard, hand-me-down furniture and kitchen storage and space-saving items cleverly utilized for nursery service. The walls were covered with a pre-pasted vinyl wall covering in patchwork squares, which is easily installed by yourself and easy to keep clean. Spare pieces of the wall covering were used to cover the doors of the white-painted cupboard, originally an unfinished piece. An old table, a hand-me-down, had one side removed and was then attached to the cupboard. Covered with selfstick laminated plastic, it makes a changing and dressing table for the baby. The rocking chair, and the floor lamp next to it, were bought at a garage sale and spray-painted white. Since storage was a necessity, kitchen items were used to make more space. Later they will be recycled to the kitchen. A revolving turntable and wall storage bin hold powders and lotions; spacemaker drawers attached under the table provide extra room for diapers and clothing; a clean-up caddy holds large bottles, medicines and hand towels. The wall-mounted holder keeps paper towels within easy reach and a large swing-top wastebasket serves as a hamper for soiled baby clothes. Final storage touch: an inexpensive laundry basket utilized as a toy chest.

This tiny guest bedroom was a complete budget decorating job, right down to the hanging of the wall covering, the making of the window shade, cube table, skirted cloth and the bedspread. Since the room was rather small and low-ceilinged, the owner selected a striped wall covering that introduces a feeling of height by visual illusion. Once this was put up, the floor was stained a light oak and given a piece of carpet. This was an unworn piece, taken from under the bed in the master bedroom which was recently recarpeted. A plain wooden cube was covered with matching wall covering as was the coordinated window shade. Home sewing projects include the bedspread in a color-coordinated diamond pattern and the cloth for the skirted table. This cloth hides a filing cabinet, used to hold an unfinished circular wood top cut to the correct size and purchased from a local lumber yard. It makes the perfect bedside table and a spot for lamp and accessories. Accessories, such as the wall-hung shelves repainted to match the color scheme, and plants and prints add a finished look to the room, which is high on good looks but cost the minimum to decorate.

BUDGET WINDOWS

There's no question about it, window shades are probably the cheapest product available today for dressing up any window in any room in your home. The ordinary little window shade has undergone vast improvements in the last decade. Now it is available in any color as well as in numerous textures and materials. Through the addition of fancy trims and pulls the plain window shade can take on extra decorative looks. Some shades are easy to laminate with fabrics through a simple iron-on method. The fabric is cut to the size of the shade, placed on top of it and then ironed. The heat from the iron releases the lamination adhesive in the shade, so that the two stick together. Laminated shades with matching draperies create a handsome effect at a window.

An ugly window can be camouflaged through the use of glass shelves built across the window close to the glass, and filled with a collection of plants and decorative glass objects.

Two screens, each one composed of two panels, can be covered with wallpaper or fabric and placed at each side of a window instead of expensive lined draperies. A plywood lambrequin, also covered in a fabric or wallpaper, is another easy and budget-minded way to frame a window effectively. Screens and lambrequins look their best and make the strongest statement when they are used in combination with window shades or sheer curtains. Vertical blinds and shutters are also relatively inexpensive today if you prefer to treat your windows with these products.

Platform seating has been popular for a long time and it was utilized to create an inexpensive budget decorating scheme in this one-room apartment. The bachelor owner wanted to divide without creating blocked-out areas within the one small room. His solution: clever divisions at floor level. He built a large platform at one end of the room, taking it up to the second window; here he positioned a smaller L-shaped platform to form a U-shaped seating area in combination with the large platform. A low false "wall," which extends to the window sill, was added at the far end of the room on top of the large platform. With the platforms and "wall" in position the owner then covered them all with inexpensive light-weight carpeting for a smooth, flowing look and integration of all the levels. His next do-it-yourself project was to make three pieces of furniture—the coffee table, the room divider and the pedestal. All are of plywood covered with the same carpeting, which also went up onto the window sill. The large platform serves for both sleeping and seating. The mattress, covered with a tailored cotton spread and topped with a mixture of cotton pillows, sees day and night time service; the divider houses the stereo and provides a spot for plants. Note how these underscore the feeling of division without loss of light. White cotton seating pads and pillows add definition and comfort in the U-shaped seating area. This area is serviced by the unique little coffee table, a plywood cube covered with carpeting and topped with a plexiglass square. The pedestal at the far end of the room adds a touch of enclosed privacy to the sleeping area and is decorated with a large plant. Three wicker cases stacked against the pedestal are not only decorative but store linens as well. Matchstick blinds were hung at the windows, chosen not only for their textural effect but their budget-wise price. The finished result is an apartment that works around the clock, decorated in a clean-lined style ideally suited to the needs of a bachelor.

BUDGET-WISE FURNITURE

There are many ways to furnish a room on a budget and do it well. You can choose from any of the following to make your task all that much easier: unfinished wood furniture; thrift and junk shop finds; low-priced modern furniture; and furniture you assemble yourself.

If you are a handy do-it-yourselfer you should make the most of the marvelous unfinished wood furniture now in the stores. This furniture happens to be well made and all it needs is finishing, which you can do yourself at home. It can be spray-painted or spray-lacquered white or a bright color. These same pieces can be covered with fabric or wallpaper for a highly individual look. Unfinished wood furniture includes chests, cupboards, armoires, end, coffee and dining tables, bookshelves, etageres and simple side chairs. It obviously has to be mixed in with some upholstered pieces, if you are utilizing it in a living room.

If you prefer the look of dark polished wood but cannot afford to buy antiques or antique reproductions, look around your local junk, thrift and second-hand shops. It is often possible to turn up good buys in these shops and usually all the furniture needs is a good polishing or perhaps a minor repair. Upholstered pieces occasionally need to be re-covered, although sometimes these can be washed or shampooed for a sparkling new appearance.

Special antiquing kits are available at paint stores and the products in the kits are easy to use to give any piece of furniture an antique finish. They can be used to update old pieces which have been stripped down or to finish the unfinished wood furniture just mentioned.

If you are not an expert do-it-yourselfer and hesitate to attempt painting or refinishing furniture, you can still furnish a room on a minimum budget.

For instance, keep your eyes scanned for furniture sales in the stores and hunt down budget buys. Ask the store salesmen to show you the latest collection of inexpensive modern furniture, as you can often find good buys which can be blended into a decorating scheme. For example, quite a few good manufacturers are now producing collections of well-designed chairs, end and coffee tables, etageres, bookshelves and dining pieces that are low in price, and so help you to save money. Clear plexiglass and plastic pieces are ideal for using in budget-wise schemes as their clear quality does not fight with other wood tones used within the scheme, and these too are low-cost items. Even certain brightly colored plastic pieces can be worked into a room for a touch of accent color.

The latest put-together furniture may appeal to you and certainly this is a money saver. Put-together furniture comes in pieces in small, easy-to-carry boxes which you can take home from the store. The pieces are quick and simple to assemble once you have them at home, and this "instant" furniture includes sofas, chairs, end and coffee tables, book-shelves and etageres. Usually made of sturdy plastic, the seating pieces are upholstered in colorful vinyl materials.

When interior designer Virginia Frankel was asked to revamp this large bed-room she faced a basic problem: the few pieces of furniture looked lost in the space and the owner could not afford to buy extra pieces. The designer skill-fully solved the problem through the utilization of paint and wall coverings. The walls above the dado were painted white, as was the ceiling. Molding at ceiling level was highlighted with green paint color-matched to the green nylon carpet. A green and white vinyl wall covering, in a trellis pattern with a

border, was carried around the room below the dado and this immediately helped to diminish the barn-like overtones of the room. A succession of floral panels, also of vinyl in soft pastels on a white ground edged with green, were positioned along the three main walls of the room. A third panel over the bed was simply attached to the wall and then highlighted with a green frame, also attached to the wall. It has the effect of a framed painting. A sheer pleated white dust ruffle and a green and white plaid spread were teamed to revitalize the bed, with plants adding extra decorative touches. This budget decorating job adds new, more furnished dimen-sions to the room for a small outlay of money. The vinyl wall covering and panels are strippable and you can easily apply it yourself, over paper, another vinyl or paint.

HOW TO SOLVE YOUR DECORATING PROBLEMS

Bright color is one of the most important decorating tools and it is particularly budget-minded since it costs no more than drab colors. It also does much to add a furnished look to any room. Interior designer Virginia Frankel adopted this tool for the multi-purpose room she designed for a teenage girl. She also made clever use of built-ins, wicker furniture and fabric. Her first job was to create an alcove for the bed and she did this on the main wall of the room by adding two-by-fours, which run from floor to ceiling on each side of the two windows. They create three distinct areas of space. The two smaller alcoves at each window were fitted out with counter tops with narrow drawers, and the insides of the top portions of the walls were lined with pegboard. Once her structural changes had been made, the designer painted the entire room bright emerald green, with a lighter apple green for the ceiling. The soft green wall-to-wall nylon carpeting echoes this color on the floor. Since she had decided that the accent colors should be pink and white, she selected a pretty floral fabric containing these tones. This was utilized for the tie-back draperies and the laminated window shades, as well as for the bed. The dust ruffle, tailored spread and four rolled bolsters turn this into a sofa for seating and lounging. Wicker pieces spray-painted bright white and flashed with bright pink cushions provide extra seating. The alcoves created by the use of two-by-fours serve for a dressing table and sewing center. They are well illuminated by the hanging fixtures and the pegboard provides space for hanging scarves, jewelry, and all manner of sewing equipment. Attractive prints and accessories add the necessary finishing touches at small cost.

Spirited contemporary design and easy-do lamination team up to create the illusion of spaciousness in this attractive one-room apartment designed by Peggy Walker on a low budget. A trio of handsome prints in a potpourri of lemon, plum and tangerine do most of the inexpensive but highly decorative job. The fabrics are laminated to plain window shades with an easy do-it-yourself process. The three-dimensional designs are alternated at the window and over storage shelves, cleverly added to provide room for all manner of items. The shades make excellent up-and-down covers whilst introducing color and pattern into the area. The table itself is yet another home carpentry project; the top, made of wood and covered with plastic laminate, simply rests on a pair of saw horses painted white. Purple-framed director's chairs, with red canvas seats and backs, fold away when not in use and were inexpensive buys. To provide sleeping facilities, the designer covered a built-in plywood platform with matching carpet and added a foam rubber mattress covered in a yellow, orange and purple print. The yellow carpet, which runs across the entire floor, is attractively balanced by cool white walls.

INEXPENSIVE ACCESSORIES

One of the easiest ways to give any room a finished look is through the use of diverse accessories. Cleverly selected accessories arranged with a degree of skill and flair help to dispense with that cold, sterile look and can often be utilized in place of costly furniture.

A plain, inexpensive chair or sofa can be highlighted with a collection of cushions in vivid colors and fabrics which add textural interest. Even a daybed in a studio apartment will take on a new appearance as a seating piece, if cushions are used on it.

Inexpensive prints, posters, lithographs and sketches are readily available and when these are framed they help dress up a plain wall to create interest within a furniture arrangment. Mirrors, wall plaques, and wall sconces can be utilized in the same manner and you can find these pieces in most stores at low prices.

The foreign-import shops carry a wide range of table-top accessories in brightly colored china or ceramics and when these are assembled within a room they add much needed color and textural interest. Also consider using colored candles, shells, mineral specimens and plants to dress up that budget-wise room.

As I pointed out at the beginning of this chapter, it is not how much you spend that really counts, but the way you use your imagination and flair. Budget-minded products that have been carefully chosen and coordinated introduce a highly decorative look, dispense with the budget mood of a room and give it a stylish ambiance.

8 · How to Update Kitchens and Bathrooms

The two rooms which seem to present the most decorating problems in any home are kitchens and bathrooms. In a sense they are decorating stumbling blocks, usually because of their size, shape and intrinsic function. Each one has its own basic needs and so has to be carefully planned and decorated so that it meets these needs—and yours.

The kitchen in particular requires extra-special attention, preferably in the early stages of decorating when you are planning room layouts and building overall schemes from scratch. Since a kitchen is a more general living area, where a variety of activities often take place—such as cooking and eating—it needs a good decorative facade as well as total efficiency. Many women spend long hours in the kitchen, preparing family needs and so on, so that it should be pleasing to be in and planned to make chores as easy as possible.

On the other hand a bathroom is not in such constant use and is a more personalized living area. Its basic requirements are an attractive appearance and good lighting.

In any event, both rooms should be well decorated with pleasing furnishings, color schemes and accessories, and as much comfort as possible. Today your task is easier than it ever was, as you have such a wealth of good new products to choose from to introduce comfort and decorative good looks. Wall coverings have been vastly improved and are now engineered to withstand cooking fumes and staining, moisture and discoloration from mildew. They are simple to put up yourself, especially the pre-pasted and pre-trimmed kind, and those made of vinyl or with vinyl finishes are sponge-cleanable. This is a major consideration as easy maintenance of these rooms is important. All of these new wall coverings work extremely well in both rooms and should be considered instead of paint, if you want a more decorated feeling.

In the same way, many floor coverings have been engineered to do well on kitchen and bathroom floors—new vinyls, linoleums and man-made-fiber carpets in particular are ideal for heavy duty areas such as the kitchen; they also do well in the bathroom as they are water repellent and many are treated to withstand moisture and mildew. Then

209

again, all the latest appliances help to introduce a modern, updated look to these rooms, so that they function efficiently and comfortably for your basic living needs.

KITCHEN PLANNING IS VITAL

More than any other room in the home, the kitchen needs to be precisely and carefully planned at the outset of your decorating. You can always rearrange furniture in a living room, but it's awfully difficult and expensive to start tearing out appliances if they have been badly positioned.

Your first consideration when you plan your kitchen layout is efficiency—and to achieve this, every appliance should be carefully placed to meet your own work needs. Each piece of large kitchen equipment should dovetail with the one adjacent to it, especially such items as the dishwasher, sink and storage cabinets, and the refrigerator, storage units and work surfaces. By carefully aligning all of these products you will create compact areas that function for specific chores and so save both time and wasted steps.

Planning the exact placement of all kitchen appliances, cabinets and work surfaces is obviously only possible if you are building a new kitchen or remodeling an existing one. If this is the case you have the opportunity to design the ideal kitchen for your needs.

Begin by making a floor plan of the kitchen, using the techniques explained earlier in this book. The floor plan shows you the exact shape of the room, indicates any architectural oddities and clarifies the amount of space available. You will also be able to visualize the best spots to position individual appliances, install cabinets and create a dining or snack area, if the space permits this.

There is no hard and fast rule which says which appliances should be adjacent to each other, but obviously some alignments are more practical than others. For example, a dishwasher should be under or close to a sink and work counter, not only to make loading easier but for the water outlet. A refrigerator needs to be close to a work surface and storage cabinets and, if possible, not immediately adjacent to the oven. If you have two good-sized walls in your kitchen, an ideal arrangement of appliances is as follows:

Wall oven, open cooking top above storage cupboards, work counter with dishwasher underneath; sink with storage cabinet below; work top. Good storage cabinets should be hung on the wall above, starting at the open cooking top and running the length of the wall. The other wall should have the refrigerator positioned at one end, with cabinets and work counters arranged next to it. If space permits you can include a snack counter with stools that push underneath.

This particular plan for placement of appliances works in both large and small or galley-like kitchens, providing you have two good walls or adjoining walls which form an L-shape to take these arrangements. You can make variations, if you wish, in the placement of items, to suit your own personal requirements. However, it's always good to remember the two points made earlier, i.e., dishwasher next to sink, refrigerator separated from the oven, for the obvious reasons of practicality.

If you are faced with an existing kitchen that is badly planned, but cannot afford to remodel, you can sometimes make corrections that help it to function with more efficiency and comfort for you. Certain appliances can be occasionally realigned without incurring lots of expense, and appliances with space in between them can be linked through the addition of work tops. Empty areas of wall space can be treated to hanging cupboards to provide additional storage, or you might include a snack counter hinged to a wall, serviced by two stools.

If you cannot make any changes in the general layout of the kitchen, either because of space or money limitations, there is no reason why you cannot give it fresh new looks. Your best tools are wall coverings, paint, floor coverings and colorful accessories.

PROBLEM: *Lack of space, storage and work surfaces; awkward architectural elements; old-fashioned equipment.*

SOLUTION: *Clever space planning plus new equipment and cabinets; inclusion of good counter space.*

The poor arrangement of cabinets and equipment plus exposed beams all helped to badly break up the space in this small kitchen with old-fashioned overtones.

The new owners of a large-sized city apartment were dismayed by the kitchen, which was not only old-fashioned looking and small but lacked good storage and work surfaces. They turned to interior designer Ving Smith, who set out to revamp the kitchen to give it more modern looks and total efficiency. After removing the old refrigerator, all the cabinets and cupboards under the sink and on the opposite wall, he set out to correct the architectural oddities near

the ceiling. He did this by adding a lowered false ceiling which runs the length of the kitchen and is set flush to the wide protruding beam. This makes the whole ceiling level and smooth looking. The ceiling was constructed out of a commercial T-track clad in mirrored copper and which supports the luminescent ceiling made of plexiglass. An extra panel of plexiglass was carried along the wide beam as facing, so that it blends with the illuminated portion of the ceiling. The designer added a strip of filler molding here to round off the ceiling treatment. With the architectural irregularities corrected, Ving Smith completed his design for the entire kitchen. Handsome wood cabinets were positioned around the walls to form a compact U-shape; matching base cupboards were placed below to add further storage space; and the L-shaped arrangement was topped with bright blue plastic laminate so that it becomes a hardy and practical work surface. A new refrigerator was purchased, the correct size to fit neatly between the cabinets. Blue and white plaid wall covering with a vinyl finish which easily wipes clean, and a blue vinyl-tiled floor add the finishing touches. With its new facade the kitchen looks and lives well, providing the ultimate in efficiency.

PROBLEM: *Lack of space, no window; old-fashioned equipment; badly marred walls.*

SOLUTION: *Precise planning; quality paneling; new appliances and a fake window.*

This typical closet-sized apartment kitchen seemed to defy good decoration. Its lack of space and badly marred walls created a cramped look, underscored by the lack of natural daylight.

Expert planning, down to the last detail, was the key to this kitchen's new handsome overtones. Rather than invest in new cabinetry, existing units above and below the sink were covered with a white high-pressure plastic laminate and an undercounter dishwasher was added. On the opposite wall, the old refrigerator was replaced with a new one, positioned further along the wall to permit the inclusion of the stove and a storage cupboard. This is balanced to the height of the stove through the addition of a butcher-block work surface. Space above the stove was utilized for a range hood to take out cooking fumes plus a small cupboard. The back wall and areas of space between cabinets were all lined with walnut plywood paneling for a smooth, sleek look; paneling also camouflages marred walls extremely well and is easy to put up yourself. Two fake windows were created through the addition of stained glass squares set in frames and hinged to the wall. They introduce a feeling of dimension and depth, while good overhead lighting fixtures dispense with the dark mood.

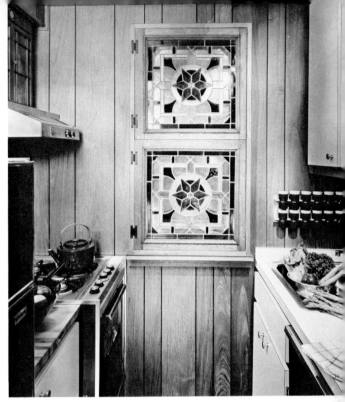

PRODUCTS FOR WALLS AND FLOORS

There are literally scores of good materials available, which you can utilize to bring new dimensions to your kitchen. Throw away any preconceived ideas about the way kitchens used to look and start with an open mind. The sky's the limit today, as far as design is concerned, and you can introduce almost any look, any ambiance you want.

Before making any decisions about how you are going to treat the walls and the floor, visit department stores and look at all the new products. In this way you will be able to ascertain which are the best for your purposes and your budget. Most are available at medium and low prices today—so that you can decorate well without its costing a fortune.

WALLS I like the look a wall covering introduces into a kitchen— color, pattern and a more furnished feeling in general. The best wall coverings to use are the specially finished wallpapers or vinyl wall coverings, as these are extremely durable, withstand steam and don't discolor. They are simple to wipe clean and keep in tip-top condition. Many of these wall coverings are pre-trimmed, pre-pasted and strippable, which makes them a snap to put up yourself. They come in a multitude of colors and patterns ranging from traditional florals to modern geometrics, with almost every other pattern in between. When using a wall covering of this type you can create a custom look by taking it up onto the ceiling and onto the doors. The smooth flow of pattern and color tends to enlarge the area, as the eye is not stopped by contrasts. Most of these wall coverings are good camouflagers, skillfully hiding cracked or badly marred walls.

Certain types of prefinished plywood paneling can be utilized in the kitchen if you want a rustic look, and of course this product also hides poor walls most successfully. Some manufacturers are now producing decorative paneling overprinted with patterns or in vivid solid colors. These make a wonderful color and design statement in any kitchen and serve as camouflagers over cracked walls. They also introduce extra insulation and soundproofing. They are easy to maintain, as they are simply sponged clean.

Many vinyl tiles go up on the wall with ease, and you have a wide selection of ceramic tile to choose from. However, this latter product is more costly and you have the price of installation as well. Once it is up, of course, it creates dazzling effects, and you can produce a real custom look if it is repeated on the floor. Ceramic tile is durable, maintains its looks well and is another easy-maintenance product. Colors and patterns are excellent.

That good old standby, paint, is another natural product for the kitchen and the paints with a lacquer finish are currently popular for creating the most up-to-date effects. If you decide to use paint, pick a bright zingy color which introduces a cheerful mood—stay away from white as it tends to create an overly sterile feeling. It also shows dirt from cooking fumes very quickly.

Paint and wallpaper (or a vinyl wall covering) are excellent decorative teammates in a kitchen and you can match up colors for a custom look.

The pattern of a wall covering helps to create the overall mood, whether it's country fresh, country rustic or traditional, or slick and modern. Interior designer Jane Victor suggests using open patterns in a small kitchen, as these help to push out the walls and so expand space by illusion. Her particular favorites for creating this effect are two-color trellis patterns, light plaids and basket-weave designs. For an old-fashioned country mood, her recommendations include florals, traditional patterns taken from old papers, patchwork or quilt patterns. In a modern kitchen she thinks that geometrics, stylized modern florals and stripes work the best, since they underscore the contemporary ambiance.

This designer also recommends carrying the wall covering onto the ceiling and the doors, when this is possible, to further expand the feeling of space and to produce a custom-designed look.

PROBLEM: *Need to demarcate dining area of a large kitchen without blocking out light, plus introduction of vivid color to counteract brick monotones; need for additional storage for china and cooking utensils.*

SOLUTION: *Use of butcher block islands for demarcation; addition of carpet for color and open bookshelves for storing china.*

The woman who lives here wanted to create a reasonably self-contained dining area at one end of her large kitchen, but her problem was to demarcate without blocking out light or cutting off the two areas from each other. Her solution was the use of two islands made of wood and covered in butcher block on top, each one positioned at angles to enclose the area. Waist high, they divide effectively and provide additional counter space. Because she likes the look of natural brick she used it extensively in the kitchen, on the walls and the floor. She soon found that this monotone play of reddish colors was dull; she needed to introduce extra-vivid hues into the area. She selected bright blue, using it on the floor by way of a piece of nylon carpeting cut to fit the exact shape of the enclosed area. She selected this particular type of man-made-fiber carpeting because it does not show the dirt and cleans easily. A serious cook, her other problem was to provide extra storage for lots of china and cooking utensils. Since she did not want to overload the back wall with more cabinets, she had to find another method of storing these items. She finally settled on a series of open-fronted bookshelves stacked on top of each other for height. These hold a mixture of blue and white and yellow china, good color accents here, plus glasses and cooking pots at the bottom. She decided to display the other cooking utensils on the bare brick wall, using large nails to hold the items. A couple of pictures, basket and wood pieces introduce a change of pace through the play of textures.

FLOORS   To my mind, vinyl tiles are by far the best product to use in a kitchen. They are available in the full color spectrum and in hundreds of patterns and textures. For instance, vinyl tiles simulate wood, parquet, planking, marble, old brick, ceramic tiles, even leather. Any of these will bring interesting textures to the floor and of course patterns include everything from Delft, Spanish and Mexican styles to contemporary geometrics. A design composed of various patterns and color combinations helps to give a kitchen floor a custom touch.

Apart from the excellence of their design, vinyl tiles and sheet vinyl are durable, resilient, retain their good looks over a long period and most importantly, they can be kept pristine very easily. Vinyl asbestos tiles are also a durable and attractive product to use in a kitchen, and these are even cheaper than pure vinyl.

If vinyl tiles do not appeal to you, there are many other products which bring color, texture and pattern to the kitchen. You have the choice of linoleum, rubber tiles, ceramic tiles, brick and all the synthetic fiber carpets engineered to work well in this heavy-duty area.

The best kitchen carpets to use are nylon, acrylic and polypropylene olefin, the latter being the best of all. Olefin fiber carpeting is usually better known as indoor-outdoor carpet, and it was first produced to be mainly used outdoors. Now that its colors and patterns are so improved it is excellent for use indoors. It is especially ideal for the kitchen because it has the lowest rate of water absorption, which makes cleaning easy. It is also stain repellent, another plus for this heavy-duty area.

WINDOW TREATMENTS

A window is part of the shell of a room and its treatment should effectively blend with or complement the background. This applies to a kitchen window as much as any other.

When decorating a kitchen window or windows, stay away from elaborate, fussy treatments. These tend to gather grime and soon become dirty and bedraggled. It is also a good idea to resist using delicate or fancy fabrics, for the same reasons. A kitchen window treatment should be practical and easy to keep clean, as well as decoratively in step with the overall scheme.

The best fabrics to use are cottons, cotton blends and synthetic fabrics, as all of these go in and out of the washing machine with ease and some of them don't even need ironing. Avoid velvets, silks, taffetas and other fabrics that must be dry cleaned.

If you do not want to use short curtains or draperies at your kitchen windows, consider window shades, wood shutters, louvered shutters or vertical blinds. All of these are trim and tailored, blend with almost any decor and are relatively simple to keep in fresh condition.

Window shades in particular are highly recommended for kitchen windows, as they can be made to fit any size and awkward shapes and are simply sponged clean of dirt, grease and grime. They give the windows a neat look and, because they come in a variety of colors and materials, they can be selected to harmonize with or accent the walls. They are the cheapest of all products to use at the windows.

PROBLEM: Small kitchen full of dark colors and wood tones; need for a place to serve snacks.

SOLUTION: Use of paint, lacquer, and cheerful wall covering and fabric; addition of a drop-leaf table.

When interior designer Nina Lee was asked to revamp this tiny suburban kitchen she was faced with what seemed to be insurmountable problems. The room seemed much smaller than it actually was because it was filled with dark colors and the colonial-style cabinets had a wood finish. The designer introduced a feeling of light airiness by painting all the cabinets white, as well as the window wall shown. The ceiling was treated to shiny white lacquer which helps to introduce a feeling of height; walls were covered with wet-look wallpaper in a geometric design featuring bright yellow, green, black, orange and pink. Washable white corduroy curtains are trimmed with braid in these same colors and the floor is stretched by visual illusion through the use of patent vinyl tiles. Because the window wall was broken by the long window seat there seemed to be no spot for a snack table—until Nina Lee devised this solution: a drop-leaf table attached under the window and to the front of the window seat, with a flap that folds down against the front when not in use. Two seat pads covered in red patent vinyl provide comfortable seating, as do the small portable stools which stack in a closet when not required.

PROBLEM: Large kitchen with old-fashioned overtones created by dated appliances, linoleum floor and white walls; need for a dining area.

SOLUTION: Total remodeling of kitchen with new equipment, floor and wall coverings; barnlike proportions reduced through use of louvered doors which also demarcate dining area.

This kitchen had plenty of potential space-wise, but it had never been updated. Old linoleum flooring, high cabinets and generally desolate air begged for creative and functional decorating assistance.

Here you can see the eating corner of the kitchen after its decorative dress-up by Virginia Frankel. The work area of the kitchen was painted white and yellow and efficiently fitted out with new appliances. The eating corner was turned into a self-contained area through ingenious decorating, all done on a medium budget. The same cushioned vinyl flooring runs through the whole area, but the designer changed the color of the walls in the dining section. These are painted a bright orange for warmth and color impact. A set of louvered doors, attached to each wall, cleverly divides the two areas of the kitchen; they are painted avocado to pick up the green touches in the vinyl as an accent color. Adding further color touches are cane chairs, each one painted a different color, partnered with a circular table. This is actually an old Victorian wrought iron base topped with wood covered in black plastic laminate. An attractive array of accessories further adds to the decorative impact of the area: Virginia has enlivened the orange wall with baskets, silver utensils and prints; hanging plants add a touch of greenery. A butcher-block shelf, jutting out from the opposite wall, provides for serving food or doubles as an extra work surface for the kitchen area, when required.

PROBLEM: *Large, drab kitchen; worn products on walls, floors and counter tops; poor window and an exposed radiator; need for dining facilities.*

SOLUTION: *A revamp with fresh paint, wall and floor coverings; addition of new furnishings.*

This kitchen of a suburban house had a drab, old-fashioned appearance and old-fashioned overtones. The poor window, exposed radiator, door opening inwards all broke up the wall without cabinets, so it seemed impossible to use furniture here. The ventilator grill set high on the wall was another unsightly element.

Obviously the kitchen needed a total revamp, but since money was a major consideration, it was redecorated rather than remodeled, at much less cost. Interior designer Elroy Edson began by covering the radiator with a built-in unit of wood fitted with a grill front and painted white. He also added a new and more modern lighting fixture on the ceiling. All the cabinets, drawers and the dado along the window wall were painted white. Attractive wall coverings then went up onto the walls and ceiling. The brown and white plaid overprinted with large white flowers helped to open up the room for an airier mood, as does the coordinated plaid on the ceiling. These are well balanced by a brown vinyl floor in a marble pattern, which adds richness and a smooth new look underfoot. All the work tops were re-covered with new brown plastic laminate for a modern look; the ugly ventilator grill was painted brown and balanced by a vivid yellow painting so that it seems much less obvious. White cotton draperies, tailored and simple in style, give the window extra importance and are in keeping with the streamlined shell. These small changes, plus the injection of strong color and pattern and the use of the latest materials, do much to update the room. To provide dining facilities, a modern white table with a plastic laminate top and chrome and vinyl scoop chairs were arranged in front of the window. These see double service in the adjoining living room when required.

PLAN FOR STORAGE

Any kitchen worth its salt contains well-planned storage. If you are building or remodeling, your problems are relatively easy to solve. You simply make a floor plan of the kitchen, showing all the storage required, and use this as a blueprint as you decorate.

The kitchen that is really hard to cope with is the one which contains little or no storage and which you cannot afford to remodel. However, even this is not hopeless. If you analyze the kitchen carefully, you will more than likely come across areas of space which can be given storage cabinets or cupboards or, at the worst, open shelves. These are usually odd portions of the walls which have been overlooked and neglected by the original kitchen planner.

By the same token, you can often utilize existing storage more fully by rearranging the items in it; you can also make use of the backs of cabinet and closet doors, on the inside, fitting them with shelves or storage planners which are readily available in the stores and which are not expensive.

Ready-made kitchen space savers, which are used in cabinets, cupboards and closets, include such things as racks for plates; carousels for cups and saucers; lazy Susan–type turntables with one and two tiers, for plates, glasses, spices, canned goods and other items; stacking bins for vegetables. There are also broom and mop holders which attach to the side walls or inside doors of closets, and other fixtures which are attached in the same spots to hold an ironing board or vacuum cleaner attachments. Sliding stacking drawers can be fitted into cupboards to hold cooking pots, while such things as cutlery trays and organizers can be utilized to keep drawers neat. All manner of small organizers to attach to the back of doors are available and include caddy-type holders for paper bags, wrapping paper, small kitchen cleaning items. These products are made by a leading manufacturer and are sold in the kitchen departments of department stores or houseware shops.

The items mentioned above and a little efficient organizing of your own will enable you to gain lots of space previously wasted. It's a good idea to remove from the kitchen all items which you don't use constantly; put them away in boxes at the back of a closet. Alternatively, put all infrequently used items in high cabinets which you find awkward to get at easily. This will free more space for items in regular use.

Interior designer Joan Blutter offers these simple ideas which can help you to gain much-needed space in your kitchen.

• Add a shelf just below the ceiling level and carry this around all the walls; use it to hold attractive cooking utensils, such as enamel or copper cooking pots, casseroles and large dishes.

• Run a narrow set of shelves down a free strip of wall to display glasses and china; or utilize the shelves for storing spices in attractive containers.

• Place glass shelves across a kitchen window close to the glass and use these to house non-perishable items in glass containers. Alternatively, fill the shelves with glasses and pretty china used frequently.

• Place a piece of pegboard painted a bright color on any available piece of wall and hang cooking utensils on it, as well as attractive small pots and pans.

• Line the inside of a door with pegboard and utilize for small cooking utensils such as whisks, cutting boards and the like.

INCLUDE ACCESSORIES

Attractive accessories should be used in a kitchen to add decorative overtones, especially if you are designing or revamping a kitchen short on space. Strategically placed accessories don't take up much room while adding a great deal of personality, plus color and textural interest.

Pretty canisters, copper utensils, old prints of fruit and vegetables, collections of ceramic dishes and old pottery or china all serve to dress up a work surface or a wall. Plants too can be included in a kitchen decorating scheme, either hung in a window area or from the ceiling. Any utensils which are attractive as well as useful can be left on display, as they add character and charm.

A word of advice: Don't clutter up the kitchen with too many accessories, as they quickly gather dust and need cleaning constantly. Always use accessories that blend well so that you produce a basic decorative theme throughout.

Finally, a word here about kitchen lighting. This is a vital element and should be carefully planned in the early stages of decorating. For proper illumination in a kitchen you need well-distributed overall light plus spots of additional light in areas where specific activities take place, such as food preparation, cooking or eating.

HOW TO SOLVE YOUR DECORATING PROBLEMS

PROBLEM: Large standard kitchen in a city apartment with no special architectural features; need for design interest to create an atmosphere.

SOLUTION: Addition of beams, new hardware and stenciled patterns on cabinets; new wall and floor coverings.

It's relatively easy to create a traditional country mood in a standard city apartment, as the owner of this one proves. Since she has always dreamed of an old-fashioned kitchen, she set about creating one here as space permitted. She began by slightly revamping the basic shell. Vinyl tiles that simulate old bricks went down on the floor; plastic beams that look real went up on the ceiling and the walls were treated to a traditional-styled wallpaper adapted from an old American stencil featuring the pineapple. The cabinets, a modern installation, were traditionalized by new black metal hardware; an enlarged version of the paper's stencil pineapple was stenciled onto the higher cupboard for clever coordination with the walls. Other old-fashioned touches include the old chandelier and an antique quilt used as a smart tablecloth. This is complemented by the old ladder-back chairs with rush seats. To further the country mood even more the owner used an antique apothecary chest as a catch-all storage piece for everything from towels to baking dishes. A tiny window valance of a fabric matched to wallpaper and accessories completes the redo—accomplished on a medium budget.

PROBLEM: L-shaped kitchen with a totally white color scheme.

SOLUTION: Redecoration with bright paint and new wall and floor coverings.

Apart from the fact that this kitchen was a peculiar shape it had a drab appearance created by a sterile white color scheme used throughout. Interior designer Abbey Darer gave it new dimensions and exciting decorative impact through the skillful use of colorful wall coverings, a color-coordinated floor and counter tops. The designer selected a large-scale, vividly colored wall covering for the utmost in impact. The green wall covering patterned with giant-sized red, blue, yellow and white flowers is pre-pasted and acrylic coated. This makes it simple to hang yourself and easy to keep pristine fresh through soap-and-water sponging. The coordinated fabric is hand-screen printed, used at the window for a smooth look on this wall. The red vinyl floor with a white border is color-coordinated to the white cabinets, which Abbey topped with red plastic laminate. For a custom look she added ceiling molding and painted this the same red, following the look through on the door trim. Since the owner needed a small snack area in the medium-sized kitchen, the designer had a simple wooden shelf attached the wall, shown in the foreground. Teamed with kitchen stools painted white and topped with cushions matched to the draperies, the little shelf becomes a handy spot for kitchen dining. Yellow and white accessories are extra decorative touches in a slick kitchen that comes alive with color.

BASICS FOR BATHROOMS

A successfully decorated bathroom has an attractive appearance, comfort and good lighting. All of these elements can be included at reasonable cost, whether you are building, remodeling or dressing up an existing bathroom.

Of course if you are building from scratch or remodeling, you can design a total bathroom that includes everything you want, right down to the latest fixtures and appliances. It is the bathroom that is simply being revamped that causes the most problems.

The most common of all difficult bathrooms is the old-fashioned type in an old building, containing outdated fixtures. White tiles, which usually appear on the walls and floor, do little to enhance the overall appearance of the room. Modern baths in suburban houses and city apartments are usually a little more appealing, as they are at least fitted out with modern fixtures. Even so they leave much to be desired, especially if they are small and windowless.

If you are faced with either kind don't despair. There are a variety of ways you can bring the ugly-duckling bathroom into line and give it decorative impact and style. You can also counteract lack of space and light through ingenuity and skillful decorating.

WAYS WITH WALLS

It is quite expensive to remove old, chipped or unattractive tiles. Apart from the cost of removing them, which usually has to be done professionally to avoid serious damage, you also have the cost of replastering afterwards.

The simplest way to deal with them is to counteract them through the use of decorative products. Most bathrooms are only tiled halfway up the wall, so that you have plenty of space above to put up a wall covering. You can easily use any of the vinyl-coated or vinyl wall coverings mentioned in the section on kitchens, as they work equally well here for all the same reasons.

A handsome wall covering introduces color and pattern into a bathroom and, when used on the ceiling and doors as well, the space is considerably expanded. Reflective or shiny wall coverings and lacquer paints are most suitable in baths, as they help to push out the walls by illusion. If you can afford it, consider using mirrored panels for all the walls or just one to stretch space; an alternative is the newest mirrored copper, which comes in panels and has been specially treated not to tarnish from moisture.

When tiles are badly damaged, you can disguise them with special tile paint which is available at most paint shops. This is simply painted on like paint, and the number of coats you require depends on the amount of the damage and how bad it is. If you prefer, you can decorate damaged tiles with stick-on vinyl tiles which are paper-thin and opaque, usually decorated in the center with a small motif. These tiles are extremely low in price and are made in standard tile sizes to fit over any tile. They have a self-stick backing and you can cover an entire wall in less than half an hour.

Certain types of wood paneling and decorative paneling may be used in a bathroom when you want to cover the entire wall—both tiles and the portions of wall above. I don't recommend the use of wood paneling on the walls above the tiles only, as this will give the room a top-heavy, unbalanced look. However, some of the decorative panelings in bright colors or pastels can be utilized in this way.

FLOOR PRODUCTS

Wall-to-wall carpeting introduces a touch of real luxury into any bathroom, however small, and today you have a good choice of synthetic fiber carpets to select from. These are the best to use for practical and maintenance reasons. Nylon, polyester, acrylic and polypropylene olefin are all hardy and withstand moisture and mildew, an important consideration in this room where water often gets splashed around. There are a variety of colors, patterns and textures to choose from today, so that you can use carpet to promote decorative good looks.

Ceramic and vinyl tiles are also suitable for a bathroom and they too effectively introduce color and pattern as well as textural effects. Vinyl tiles are moderately priced; ceramic tiles are more expensive.

In combination, wall coverings and floor coverings do much to distract the eye from ugly old fixtures which you cannot afford to replace with newer styles. If you wish, however, old tubs and washbasins with exposed pipes can be somewhat disguised through the use of built-in surrounds made of wood. The surrounds can be painted or lacquered a strong color, or alternatively covered with a wall covering, a wallpaper or mirrored copper. Obviously this is quite expensive to do, unless you are an expert home carpenter.

PROBLEM: Old-fashioned bathroom with white tiles on walls and floor; unattractive window; old fixtures.

SOLUTION: Utilization of bright paint, plus new vinyl floor, colorful shower curtain, linens and accessories.

This bathroom, like most in old city apartments, lacked personality. Stark white everywhere accentuated old fixtures.

The young career girl who occupies the apartment containing this bathroom asked interior designer Virginia Frankel to give it new decorative life. Since money was a problem she was prevented from removing the white tiles and unattractive fixtures which would have been costly to replace. Working on the premise that bright color often works wonders, she began by painting the walls above the tiles a vivid green. To make the exposed pipe less obvious she painted the upper portion green, the lower part white so that it blends into the wall. To camouflage the old floor, Virginia put down blue cushioned vinyl that introduces color, comfort and a sleek look underfoot. The solid rafts of blue and green in the room are carried over onto the shower curtain, which skillfully hides the ugly bath, and in the towels. Virginia's decorative solution for the tiny window was beads, in alternate colors of white, green and blue. They hide the frosted glass but don't block out the light. A white bath mat, toilet-seat cover plus plants and prints add extra touches of accent color and decorative highlights that pull the eyes away from the unattractive white tiles.

PROBLEM: *Tiny cramped bath with marred walls and awkward architectural elements at ceiling level; old-fashioned fixtures.*

SOLUTION: *Mirrored copper to sheath cracked walls and introduce spaciousness by visual illusion; built-ins also sheathed in copper to camouflage ugly old fixtures; dropped false ceiling.*

Interior designer Ving Smith brought a clutch of clever ideas together to create new and exciting dimensions in this tiny bathroom. Architectural irregularities at ceiling level were first camouflaged through the use of a dropped, false ceiling made out of a large panel of plexiglass and illuminated from behind. All of the cracked walls were slickly hidden behind panels of mirrored copper that produce reflective, shimmering effects in the tiny area and expand it by optical illusion. The bath and the washbasin were boxed in with wood surrounds, also sheathed in copper; these serve to unify the total area and also hide old fixtures. Handsome brass towel rail and brass-and-crystal lighting fixture add the finishing touch.

ACCESSORIES ADD IMPACT

Accessories should be given their full play in a bathroom, for the very obvious reason that they help to create strong decorative impact.

Bath linens and shower curtains, which I am including in the accessory category, do a lot to cheer up a drab bathroom or add accent colors in a freshly revamped one. A shower curtain is very useful for disguising an old-fashioned tub, especially if it is full length, so that the tub is completely hidden. Shower curtains now come in every color of the rainbow, a variety of patterns and material, so that you no longer have to put up with dreary opaque plastic hanging around the tub. You can usually match up bath linens to the shower curtain for a coordinated custom look; if you wish, you can use a patterned shower curtain and solid color bath mat and towels for a change of decorative pace. It's a good idea to avoid mixing two patterns together, especially if the bathroom is small.

Plants are living accessories very popular for use in bathrooms today and of course they flourish well because of the damp and steamy atmosphere. These can be displayed on wall-hung shelves or hung from the ceiling, depending on your personal taste and the other accessories used. Attractive prints, posters, and paintings, colorful glass or pottery jars and decorative items add a fillip to walls, shelves, bath and washbasin areas, so be sure to include them in your revamp.

A good mirror is necessary and strong lighting is vital. In a small bathroom you can usually add lighting over the mirror above the washbasin and make do with that. In a larger bathroom you will need to include a central ceiling fixture or wall sconces, so that enough light is evenly distributed.

Storage is important in a bathroom, but it is not always possible to include very much, especially in tiny baths. Often the only storage possible in the available space is the medicine chest over the sink. When this is the case, look for wall space where you can add shelves for extra toilet articles, such as perfume and pretty containers holding small items. If you need an extra shelf or two for towels and bath linens, you can add one in the bath area, either on the long wall or the end wall opposite the shower attachment. Glass shelves look the prettiest and because of their see-through, colorless quality they appear to take up little room.

If you have an old-fashioned bathroom and more than the average amount of space, an antique chest or an unfinished wood chest painted a gay color is a useful and handsome addition. When a standing mirror

is used with it, the chest becomes an extra dressing table and of course
the drawers are perfect for storage.

Some of the photo stories in this chapter illustrate how unattractive,
old-fashioned and small bathrooms have all been ingeniously updated
and given decorative impact. Most of the ideas can easily be adapted to
suit your own living needs.

PROBLEM: *Small bathroom in a modern apartment which needed a strong decorative scheme to
introduce interest.*

SOLUTION: *New checked wallpaper and paint; area rug and accessories.*

This modern bathroom in a new high rise was full of up-to-the-minute ideas, such as the round tub
and the handsome built-in vanity. But there were no strong architectural features in the room and it
had a bland uninteresting look. The bachelor owner created a striking effect at small cost, simply
through the use of a silver and black wall covering and strip molding, plus black and white paint.
The walls were first covered with the wall covering and trimmed with the black-painted strip
molding used at intervals around the tub area and on portions of the adjoining wall and the window
wall. the vanity was painted black, the doors white. A white fake-fur rug and white window shades
were other additions that help to highlight the black and white scheme. Attractive accessories and
the scoop chair complete the scheme.

PROBLEM: Large bath with old-fashioned fixtures, ugly window and exposed radiator; chipped tiles on floor.

SOLUTION: The use of paint, fabrics and carpeting plus addition of chest and mirror.

The bath in this turn-of-the-century house was sterile and tired looking. Old fixtures, tiled walls and floor plus an unattractive window all teamed together to create a desolate mood.

This large bathroom had lots of space but was short on decorative impact. This was quickly introduced by the new owners, through the use of some clever decorating ideas in the easy revamp that was also easy on the pocketbook. The ceramic tiles were left intact, as it would have been too costly to remove them and then to replaster. But the wallpaper above was stripped and a towel rail removed. The walls were then painted deep green. This made the ideal background for the crisp green and white floral print generously used for both the window draperies and the shower curtains and valance. The full-length draperies on a rod give the window balance and sheer curtains ensure privacy and camouflage the unattractive radiator. White grosgrain ribbon was used for tie-backs on both shower curtain and draperies. A green shag rug completes the decorative redo, adding color and comfort while hiding the chipped tile floor. Since there was plenty of space the owners used an antique chest and mirror to add a furnished look and provide storage for linens.

PROBLEM: *Large bathroom in an old house which needed total remodeling.*

SOLUTION: *New tub in a raised platform, plus new built-in vanity; use of paneling and plastic laminate.*

A large bathroom in an old house was spacious and light, but it was unusable because of its badly marred walls, floor and the ancient fixtures. Interior designer Abbey Darer was brought in to remodel. She began by tearing out all the old fixtures. Her next step was to build the step-up platform to surround the bath, a new purchase. Made of sturdy wood, the platform was sheathed in light-colored plywood paneling. Abbey used this to cover a shelf along the back wall and to line the alcove wall into which she had fitted a new two-basin vanity. Doors of the vanity and the valances in front of the concealed strip lighting were also lined with the paneling. To highlight the silvery wood tones of the paneling, the designer lined the back wall and inside the vanity alcove with a black plastic laminate that simulates slate. A white vinyl floor completed the remodeling job. For touches of accent color, Abbey used plants, prints, small decorative accessories and green and white towels. The old-fashioned window was hidden by sliding shoji screens.

9 · Decorating Ideas for Children's Rooms

Rooms for children, whatever their ages, need as much careful thought and planning as any other room in a home. Four things are of major importance in a youngster's room: durability, ease of maintenance for hygiene, comfort, and an attractive ambiance.

Children, just like adults, respond to colors and attractive furnishings and their own rooms should come alive with bright, zingy tones and patterns, good looking furniture and appropriate accessories.

It's a good idea to let older children, especially teenagers, participate in the decoration of their own private abodes. Most children have their own ideas about how they want their rooms to look and have favorite colors and favorite things they want to include. With your guidance they can create their own decorative environment—one which will please them and satisfy their own particular living needs.

When you shop for products, seek out all of those which are going to be durable and resilient when exposed to childish wear and tear—floor and wall coverings that will bear up well under lots of abuse and are easy to maintain; fabrics with a special finish to repel soiling and staining; furniture with natural wood or plastic laminate–covered surfaces, which won't mark easily.

If you are decorating for a pre-teen child select furniture that grows with the child, so that it can be used in later years without appearing to be overly juvenile. There is a wide range of this furniture on the market today and it includes beds, desks, bookcases and storage units which see good service for six- and seven-year-olds yet continue on into the teen years.

This furniture, usually in natural wood tones, bright painted finishes or covered with plastic laminates, blends into any background, so that all you have to do is change the decorative overtones of the basic shell as the child grows. Let's look at some of the best products to use for children's rooms, ones which fall into the medium-price category.

FLOORS

Carpeting is about the best material to put down on the floor for several reasons. It adds comfort, warmth and is a good soundproofer in a room for children of any age. It also cushions falls, a point to consider if you are decorating a nursery. The synthetic carpets are a good bet in juvenile quarters for all their wearing and easy-upkeep qualities. They are very durable, repel staining remarkably well, hide dirt and can be easily cleaned with suds and water. Colors are literally multitudinous—pastels, clear bright colors and hot or warm shades; patterns are just as numerous, from all the usual geometrics and plaids to nursery-rhyme scenes and the like.

It's advisable to select a pattern for a child's room, as patterned carpet shows the least amount of dirt; it also introduces extra design interest underfoot. If you cannot afford broadloom carpet running wall to wall, look at the latest carpet tiles. Generally made of nylon, they can be put down to resemble a wall-to-wall carpet and you can create imaginative effects by combining different colored squares or squares with different patterns. Since they have foam rubber backing they dispense with the need for an underlay; some come with self-adhesive backing which means you can lay them yourself and so save the cost of installation.

Vinyl tiles and vinyl asbestos tiles are other good products to use, as these too are resilient, hard-wearing and easy to mop clean. Most good vinyls also retain their sheen without waxing. Because there is an extensive range of colors and patterns in vinyl and vinyl asbestos tiles you can produce exciting effects to delight the eye of a child. Cushioned-vinyl flooring, in sheets, and linoleum and rubber also produce similar results in a room and are practical to use. If you wish, you can put down an area rug in combination with vinyl, for added warmth, texture and color, but always be sure the rug is backed with a non-skid tape to prevent slips and falls.

Plain wood floors are always handsome, but after staining and waxing treat them to a few coats of clear polyurethane varnish, as this adds a sheen, prevents scuffing and so cuts down on maintenance. The varnish also prevents accidents from wood splinters, as it seals the floor.

Painted wood floors are colorful for children's rooms; particularly if you have decorated the painted background with a stenciled pattern in a contrasting color. Interior designer Joan Blutter suggests painting colorful story-book characters all over the floor, if you are a dab hand with a paintbrush. She recommends that all painted wood floors be coated with at least six coats of clear polyurethane varnish.

PROBLEM: *Lack of space in a small room to be shared by two boys; need for two beds plus storage, study and play space; total ease of maintenance required.*

SOLUTION: *A closet remodeled to hold two bunk beds; wall-hung shelves for toys; two long wall units combining storage and desks; child-proof materials for easy upkeep.*

Interior designer Jane Victor wanted to create a stimulating color scheme in this room to be shared by two boys. Since their favorite color was fire-engine red she built the scheme around this, adding two shades of blue and solid rafts of white for accent. Patterns were also utilized to highlight the overall scheme. Her other problem was to turn inadequate space into a self-contained haven for the two boys, which they could happily share for studying, playing and sleeping. Her first task was to remodel a large closet into sleeping quarters. She did this by removing the doors and adding two bunk beds. The inside back wall was papered with a blue and white geometric; the side walls were painted red to match the plywood front containing "entrance holes" to the beds, reached by way of the blue ladder. The same red flashes over the ceiling and reappears in the red and blue vinyl floor cleverly designed with strips of vinyl that produce an eye-catching, dimensional effect. The same blue and white fabric appears on the wall above the double storage chest, which is roomy enough to hold clothes for both boys. A contrasting fabric of red, white and blue is utilized on panel tracks at the windows. Jane selected this window treatment because it is tailored and efficient and does not crowd the room as a more elaborate treatment might have. Plexiglass shelves store and display toys; plexiglass chairs service the long double-desk unit on the opposite wall. Light bulbs on the ceiling are practical and fun, and supplement hanging lights over the desks. Red, white and blue vinyl cushions provide extra seating without taking up space. Floor, walls and all furniture surfaces are wipe-clean; fabrics have a special finish to counteract soiling and staining.

Here you can see the other side of the eye-catching boys' room. Light blue has a softening effect over the long double-desk unit painted white. This also contains drawer space and extra toy storage areas. More plexiglass shelves hold treasures; personal, bright red bulletin boards service each child's needs. The clothes closet at the end of the room is decorated with vinyl cut-outs simulating balloons, in all the colors used in the room.

WALLS

There are innumerable wall coverings on the market that add zest and uniqueness to children's rooms. Apart from all the usual patterns, such as stripes, plaids, florals and geometrics, there are highly decorative juvenile patterns available today. Patchwork and quilt designs, Raggedy Ann and nursery-rhyme characters, animal prints and toy soldier parades are just a few of the marvelous patterns readily available in wallpapers and other wall coverings such as vinyls, vinyl-backed and vinyl-coated products. These products with a special protective finish are ideal for toddlers' rooms, since finger marks and crayon sketches are removed with ease, and the papers and wall coverings are durable and hard to damage. They retain their good looks and sponge clean with ease.

I can't stress the importance of ease of maintenance enough. This is necessary to promote total hygienic conditions, especially vital in a nursery. So always look for those products for walls and floors that clean quickly, and which actually help to make your life all that much easier, too.

Paint is always a good standby product, but this doesn't resist soiling as much as wall coverings, and of course it is sometimes difficult to remove crayon marks without discoloring the paint itself. If you prefer to utilize paint, which is certainly one of the more budget-minded products available, look at the latest lacquers in bright colors as they are not only highly decorative but hard-wearing too.

Fabric and sheets make wonderful wall coverings in a child's room and are easy to attach with adhesive or a staple gun. Interior designer Angelo Donghia has created some beautiful effects in children's rooms using sheets of his own design as his chief decorative element. He has often lined walls with them and then carried over matching sheets onto windows, the bed and upholstered furniture. This promotes a custom-decorator look and of course this type of scheme is relatively easy to put together, as you don't have to worry about matching up diverse patterns and colors. Angelo recommends the following method of hanging sheets on walls: Add a narrow strip of molding or plain wood at floor and ceiling levels all around the room and attach sheets to wood, using small tacks. Hide the tacks or nails with glued-on braid trim. This method makes quick removal of sheets for washing relatively easy.

Interior designer Jane Victor, a young mother herself, has these suggestions for wall treatments for children's rooms:

    • Cut out nursery-rhyme characters from a well-illustrated book and paste them onto a wall painted a contrasting solid color. Varnish the wall several times to seal down cut-outs and add a gloss.

• Carry cork tiles over an entire wall and use this as a giant-sized bulletin board in a teen-ager's room. It works for a girl or a boy—they can pin on their favorite things and photographs or magazine pictures of their favorite people.

• Cover a wall with felt for the same effect and use this as a backdrop for family photographs or movie and sports idols.

• Buy a large-scale map of the world and attach this to a wall, surrounding it with pieces of molding to simulate a frame. These maps are available from book or specialty stores and teen-agers find them interesting, especially if they have had foreign vacations.

• Run narrow shelves across a wall, up to the ceiling; use them to display and store toys or favorite things.

• Cover a wall with a hand-painted mural of a nursery-rhyme scene or any other scene, if you are clever enough with a paint brush. Paint supergraphics on a teen-ager's bedroom wall, or let the child do it if capable.

Wood paneling is a good product to use in an older child's haven, especially a boy's room. You can find plywood paneling that comes pre-trimmed and pre-cut to the size of the room and which is relatively simple to put up yourself. Certain brands of this type of paneling are now available in the medium-price range.

OTHER FURNISHINGS

As pointed out before, a window is an integral part of the background of any room. It should be carefully treated to blend in with the walls, or introduce contrast in color, design, texture and pattern.

The window treatment you select for a child's room depends on the overall decorative scheme of the room. For example, in a girl's room filled with pretty fabrics and delicate colors, soft draperies or tie-back Priscilla curtains are the best solution. A boy's room full of tailored overtones should be given shutters or louvers, tailored draperies or window shades.

Nurseries always require good room-darkening window treatments, and even if you use draperies or shutters, consider including window shades. Most of these have room-darkening qualities, especially essential for afternoon naps. Window shades come in all colors and textures today and you can use them to promote a smooth look between windows and walls.

As a matter of fact, it's a good idea always to include a window shade in children's rooms, because of their intrinsic room-darkening assets. If you are utilizing other materials for the basic treatment, select a simple shade that does not compete. Most shades are moderately priced and they are simple to keep clean. If you plan to use fabrics, select those that are durable and treated to withstand soiling, or which launder easily. Avoid using fabrics which have to be constantly dry cleaned, as this does become expensive.

FURNITURE   You can furnish a child's room on a relatively small budget, particularly if you use budget-wise modern furniture, wicker or unfinished wood furniture you paint yourself. Brightly lacquered furniture adds color and life to any room and is certainly appealing to a child.

Tables, desks, bookshelves, storage chests and cubes are just a few of the items made of unfinished wood, which you can lacquer in bright red, yellow, green, blue or any other color you choose, to suit the overall scheme. The beauty of this furniture is that it can be revamped with fresh paint later, to suit the child's tastes as he or she grows. This same furniture can also be covered with fabrics, wallpapers, wall coverings or vinyl upholstery fabrics, for a different look. These are easily attached with special adhesives. When matched to walls or fabrics used elsewhere in the room, they produce that coordinated, custom-designed look.

When selecting other kinds of furniture it is wise to buy certain pieces which grow with the child, such as storage chests, desks, tables, chairs and bookshelves which can all be retained. This means that you only have to replace the crib with a bed at a later stage.

ACCESSORIES   Every room needs accessories to give it personality and individuality and a child's room is no exception. In a nursery your basic accessories will be toys of course, plus attractive prints and pictures on the walls. Later these can be replaced with the child's favorite things, those little personal possessions that mean so much to a growing youngster.

In a room for an older child you can use other treasured items and toys as accessories, displayed in cabinets or on open bookshelves. Books themselves should be given room space and are best housed on wall-hung shelves or free-standing units. These are readily available in plastic, wicker or wood and are not all that expensive. A giant-sized bulletin board or a wall of cork makes an ideal backdrop for accessories, photographs and memorabilia; sports equipment and trophies can be shown off to advantage on shelves, wall-hung to save floor space.

Posters, prints, maps, pennants and photographic blow-ups are also suitable for dressing up a wall—let the child use his or her imagination in hanging and grouping these items, so that the room grows in individuality and personal charm.

Finally, a word here about color. Children find color stimulating and exciting. They are as responsive to it as adults are and it can be used to create a special mood and an ambiance in their own private havens. Let them select their own colors, providing the combinations are suitably matched and do not clash. Like everyone else they know which colors they are happiest around, so don't attempt to inflict your own tastes. In this way they will feel that their rooms are really and truly their own.

PROBLEM: Large room for two children requiring sleeping quarters for two and a feeling of more warmth.

SOLUTION: Addition of bunk beds and a rich color scheme.

Interior designer Virginia Frankel brought totally new dimensions to this nursery through the use of an unusual carpet and lots of strong, warm color. The formerly all-white room, somewhat drab and uninteresting, was immediately perked up and became a fun place for children to sleep and play. The entire color scheme and theme of the nursery playroom draws its inspiration from the whimsical carpet, patterned all over with patchwork pieces and Raggedy Ann and Andy characters. The yellow, orange, blue, gold and greens are repeated throughout the room. Virginia painted the walls a bright orange for a warm, stimulating effect. Built-in bunk beds were painted vivid yellow and both beds were given tailored spreads. The slide was lined with matching blue vinyl. Raggedy Ann cutouts decorate the window wall, while cube tables and miniature chairs furnish other areas. The carpet has a foam backing and anti-static control; its soil-hiding properties and wearability make it ideal for a heavy-traffic children's room.

HOW TO SOLVE YOUR DECORATING PROBLEMS

PROBLEM: *Nursery short on space which also had to be furnished on a limited budget; need for storage and work surfaces, easy-to-clean materials.*

SOLUTION: *Built-ins, window shades and a fabric-covered floor.*

This nursery with small dimensions was skillfully decorated by Carl Fuchs, to provide all the facilities for a new-born baby. Storage and work surfaces were major considerations in the room, which also had to be decorated on a small budget. The designer created an ample storage area at the window side of the room, using an unfinished wood built-in composed of two spacious cupboards and two sets of pull-out drawers. Counter space above is utilized for changing baby and to store and display toys. The built-in was painted white as crisp contrast against sunny yellow walls, and Carl Fuchs added decorative looks through the fabric pasted onto doors and drawer fronts. This yellow, tangerine and coffee striped cotton-and-synthetic blend was also laminated onto the window shades. It reappears on the tailored valance and the narrow panels which add extra linear interest at the two windows. Another cotton-and-synthetic blend fabric, this time a plaid in the same colors, was stretched across the floor, attached with adhesive and varnished with clear polyurethane several times. This is an inexpensive and practical idea for the floor in this light traffic room. The fabric was repeated as a spread on the junior bed, for coordinated good looks. For additional efficiency above the changing surface, the designer put up a roomy shelf for powders and lotions, plus a towel rail immediately below. Wicker chair, wicker lamp and small plastic table were inexpensive additions which help to round out the room.

PROBLEM: *Boy's room, short on space, required to function as bedroom-den; need for lots of storage and work surfaces.*

SOLUTION: *Utilization of built-ins and clever division of space.*

Getting the most out of a small amount of space was the basic problem in this tiny room for a teenage boy, especially since he had lots of clutter and personal treasures to display and store. The solution was use of some clever built-ins and unfinished wood furniture painted bright blue and white. The shell was treated first. The walls were painted white and the floor was covered with a blue and red plaid carpet made of nylon. Instead of a box spring for the mattress, a base was made of wood and fitted with two roomy drawers for storage. A headboard was created by placing a blue and white painted chest at the head of the bed, the drawers facing toward the end wall. This holds clothes and makes a spot for a reading lamp and clock. Unfinished wood chests, also painted blue and white, and a table top on saw horses combine to produce the desk and extra storage at the window end. Wall-hung shelves house books, radio and sports equipment. A giant bulletin board above the bed is both practical and decorative. Such things as a kitchen chair and a small occasional table partnered with vinyl cushions complete the budget-wise decorating scheme, which is filled with easy-upkeep materials and services all the needs of a young man.

PROBLEM: *Small budget for revamping a teenager's room short on furniture and decorative interest.*

SOLUTION: *Clever window treatment; budget-wise accessories and furniture; paint and fabric.*

New shocking pink carpet and striped wall covering had depleted the budget for this teenager's room. The rest of it had to be completed on a relatively small budget. Since the bed and two end tables were the only pieces of furniture in the room, interior designer Virginia Frankel used ingenuity and imagination to produce a more charming and decorative effect. She treated the window to a "box" created from four boards each 18″ wide, cut to fit window, painted white and affixed to the wall. The "box" frames the window and doubles as a dressing table, complete with spacemaker drawers (normally used in a kitchen) fitted underneath. An inexpensive polyester fabric was the designer's choice for the draperies, cafe curtains, bedspread and pillow sham. The pretty green, yellow and white floral is a cool accent against the hot pink nylon carpeting. An unfinished wood Parsons table and two natural-colored wicker chairs were all painted white, as were the two existing tables. They help to add a furnished look at small cost, as do the paper flowers used to dress up the wall behind the bed and the window, purchased for a few dollars at a novelty store. A plate rack for books is a practical and inexpensive idea. Plants, pretty lamps and other small accessories add finishing touches in a room that works as a comfortable haven for a teenager.

PROBLEM: *A small room which had to function as a bed-sitting room for a teenage girl; need for good seating, storage and desk.*

SOLUTION: *Use of pastel and white color scheme and white wicker furniture to expand feeling of space.*

Interior designer Nina Lee's basic problem in this teenage girl's room was creating an ambiance for entertaining and studying as well as sleeping. Lack of real space meant utilizing the bed as a seating piece as well; she also had to include storage and a desk without crowding the room. The young occupant expressed a liking for soft pastel hues, yellow in particular, so Nina used this color as the springboard. The floor was covered with a pale yellow carpet, carried wall-to-wall to expand floor area by visual illusion, and provide comfort and soundproofing. A white wallpaper over-patterned with pink, yellow, orange and pale green in an airy lattice design helps to push walls out and adds dimension. Nina gave the windows white painted louvered shutters to produce a tailored look in the room. Straight-lined, simple white wicker furniture was selected for the same reason, as the teenager had requested no frills and flounces. The handsome bed, fitted with a tailored spread and bolsters, sees double duty as a sofa; its tailored spread picks up the colors from the wallpaper, as do such things as the rocking chair cushion, lamp and the pictures on the wall. Balancing the bed are a storage chest which sees service as an end table, the bookcase, storage cube table and the rocker. The cheval mirror updated with wicker is a charming touch and just the thing a young girl appreciates. The white lacquered desk, part of it visible in the foreground, was placed against the opposite wall, to leave traffic space in the center of the room. Nina Lee recommends wicker for children's rooms because it has a light, airy appearance, is budget-minded and it can grow with the child. All materials have easy maintenance qualities.

10 · Decorating for a Man

Designing a room for a man is no more difficult than any other decorating job. In fact, you tackle it in much the same way as you would more general living areas, as outlined earlier in this book.

You should make a good, detailed floor plan and use it as a blueprint through all stages of decorating. It not only clarifies available space, but points up the best way to arrange furniture and create a focal point. It defines how much furniture you can comfortably include and so acts as a shopping guide.

Once you have the floor plan in hand, it's a good idea to ascertain the occupant's tastes in all areas of decorating. Establish color preferences, wood tones preferred, style of furniture and the actual pieces required. It is also important to find out which wall and floor coverings and fabrics a man likes the most, the textures and patterns he finds compatible. All of these elements contribute to the interior environment and it should be one in which he feels relaxed and comfortable. You should also make a checklist of all the items required to suit the activities of the room and the man's actual living needs. This will help you to create comfortable furniture arrangements that work successfully. And don't forget, most men hate fussy bric-a-brac cluttering up surfaces, and small delicate pieces of furniture which are easily overturned, so try to banish these from your overall decorative plan. However, if he has lots of memorabilia or collections, books and records, plan to include all of these items, especially if it is a room such as a den which is for his exclusive use. In this case it should reflect his individuality and personal tastes.

COLOR SCHEMES

Most men have quite strong color preferences and you must use colors they respond to in a room designed for them.

Strong vital color combinations such as red and blue, red and black, red and brown, black and white, and brown and beige please many men, while others go for the softer natural colorations like stone, cement and sand; some feel more comfortable with earth and autumnal schemes based on a play of rich golds, terra cottas, tan and brown. White accented with bright colors is popular, on the other hand few men feel happy around delicate pastels such as baby pinks and blues, so stay away from these.

The best way to build a color scheme for a man is to have him collect swatches of wall and floor coverings and fabrics plus paint chips in a variety of different colors so that he can show you his favorite colors. Together you can create a suitable scheme.

I have found that most men feel comfortable in a room based on a play of one color highlighted with an accent color, or a room built around two or three colors. These color combinations are restful and do not jar on the nerves or distract the eye. Lots of colors together tend to create a busy look and anyway these schemes are difficult to handle successfully, so avoid them.

Don't forget that almost all bright colors look and live their best when highlighted with black, white or a combination of these two. They are neutrals which bring out other colors so that they are shown to their advantage.

Interior designer John Elmo offers these tried and tested color schemes for men:

Royal Blue used as the basic color, accented with beach plum and lots of white highlights. *Brown* over major areas, highlighted with sand or beige tones plus ultramarine. *Forest Green* for the walls, accented with white and crimson; the same green accented with black and white; alternatively, with black and crimson. *Sand* or *Cement* tones for all major areas accented with brick red, small touches of brown. A play of *Grays* from light to dark for the entire room, accented with lemon yellow and silver; all-gray scheme accented with chrome, silver and metallic tones plus a bluish-purple. *White* for the walls, balanced by black, plus black and white patterns and a touch of clear red in small splashes.

VISUAL ELEMENTS

PATTERNS   If you want to use patterns in a man's room, be sure you don't include too many which create a busy, crowded look. Select strong, large-scaled or dominant patterns, as these usually appeal to

245

men most. It's generally best to avoid the use of tiny or minutely-scaled patterns, pretty florals and such because they may strike men as too fussy. But some men like small patterns, and since you are doing this together you'll know. Geometrics, plaids, tartans, checks, stripes, and some documentary prints are your best choices. Always make sure the patterns in a room suit the overall decorative style of the room. For instance, traditional patterns look best with antiques or period-style furniture; geometrics and abstracts with modern pieces. If you are using patterned materials for walls, draperies or upholstery, then add balance with a solid-color floor covering or vice versa.

TEXTURES All textures make a statement in a room, just like patterns, and they should be chosen with care and thought. Men like strong or plain textures, so consider all the smooth wools, tweeds, corduroys, suede, leather, vinyls that simulate suede and leather, heavy velvets, linens and cottons. It is advisable to dismiss such textures as silks, satins, light-weight fabrics or sheer fabrics, although the latter can be used at windows in combination with a heavier fabric.

STYLES AND FINISHES Most men like natural wood tones, whether these are light, bleached oaks and pine or the darker colors from walnut through to mahogany, teak and ebony. Steel-and-glass pieces are also popular, along with certain brightly colored plastic pieces or clear plexiglass. Accent pieces of wicker, cane and bamboo appeal to some men, especially when these are left in natural tones.

However, the majority of men feel uncomfortable with furniture painted in delicate pastel colors, or items which have been treated to gold or silver finishes. On the other hand, Chinese lacquered antiques are quite popular, because they have a strong masculine look. These make a striking statement in a room.

WALL COVERINGS

You have a vast choice of wall coverings for a man's room, whether it's a bedroom, den, office, library, hobby room, or bathroom.

Paneling is a favorite in all wood tones, as are suede and leather or the new vinyls that simulate these materials. Certain fabrics are perfect for a man's haven—in particular corduroy, velvet, linen, heavy cotton, flannel, wool, tweeds, hopsack, and twill.

Wallpaper and vinyl wall coverings can be utilized to cover the walls, but if you decide to put these up always choose strong, dominant patterns or those with an embossed or self-pattern. Paint makes the scene with ease, as in all rooms in the home and brightly colored lacquers are especially popular.

Cork tiles and some of the new decorative panelings create interesting effects, and like wood paneling and fabric they are ideal for covering up badly marked walls. They are also insulators and soundproofers.

PROBLEM: *Executive office requiring work and relaxation areas; need for clever division of space.*

SOLUTION: *Carefully grouped furniture and use of occupant's favorite navy blue and browns, plus inclusion of his art collection and plants.*

The executive who works in this office asked interior designer Virginia Frankel to create a mood of gracious elegance in his working environment. He also wanted her to introduce individuality through the use of his art collection, plants and his favorite colors—blue and brown. His other request was for a relaxation area as well as efficient working space. The designer began by lining the walls with navy blue felt, which she highlighted with molding painted white and white vertical blinds at the two windows. The acoustical felt was also employed on the ceiling for extra soundproofing and harmony. To underscore the blue felt walls she used wall-to-wall carpet in a mixture of blue and walnut checks; the nylon carpeting was chosen for its no-shock characteristics and durability, as well as its good looks. With the shell in place, the designer used a major grouping of furniture, composed of a modern walnut desk, tan leather desk chair and tan sofa. The sofa was placed flush to the desk but faces the bookcase wall. A coffee table and chair complete the seating area, created for relaxation. The occupant's collection of primitive sculptures and modern art is ranged around the room, the sculptures mainly wall-hung for convenience as well as striking effects. These are underscored by lots of plants, specially requested by the executive. To provide extra color and design interest in the room, and also house such things as books, a radio and bar, Virginia Frankel created a built-in unit on the wall facing the sofa. This was achieved through the remodeling of two closets.

HOW TO SOLVE YOUR DECORATING PROBLEMS

PROBLEM: *Tiny room which had to function as a study-bedroom; need for storage of books, records and hi-fi equipment.*

SOLUTION: *Clever manipulation of wall space; use of sleep sofa and matching love seat; plus pale color scheme.*

A small bedroom was turned into a study as well, by Bebe Winkler and Bob Patino. The owner, a music lover, also needed to house a collection of records, hi-fi equipment and books, plus clothes. The designers made the most of every inch of space. The long wall, traditionally used for the bed, was appropriated for the wall-length rosewood and plastic laminate storage piece. This suavely obviates the need for closets, dressers, desk, storage and shelf space. Dual-purposefulness shows its face in the window treatment as well. Off-center windows with no view, plus a radiator, appeared to be almost insurmountable obstacles for good design. But ceiling-hung, wall-to-wall shade cloth vertical blinds came to the rescue. They rotate to let in the proper amount of light and air, while concealing the brick wall across the court. They camouflage the air conditioner and radiator, without interfering with their function. They also hide a hi-fi speaker. To block out the last vestiges of light when desired, room-darkening window shades were added. A love seat on the wall opposite the storage unit opens up to become a bed; it was partnered with a matching stationary love seat which provides additional seating. They are in the same soft beige tones as the carpeting, which was carried across the floor, up the walls and onto the ceiling to turn the room into an attractive soundproofed cocoon. A brown and white area rug adds texture and design interest on the floor. Color accents are introduced with books and pillows, plus a grouping of plants not shown in the picture.

Here you can see the room with the vertical blinds closed. They promote a sleek, tailored look with linear overtones on the window wall.

PROBLEM: *Small room needing to be revamped as a den-study; necessity for lots of storage space and display shelves plus furniture arrangement for TV watching.*

SOLUTION: *Use of a wall-hung furniture system to free floor space and provide required storage-display space; furniture grouping facing television set.*

The man who lives here wanted a room of his own where he could enjoy his favorite hobbies—reading and listening to music—as well as watch television comfortably. Apart from providing for these living needs, he asked designer Peggy Walker to include lots of storage for papers and files. Her solution: a wall-hung system of furniture, carefully spaced around two walls to provide the best in looks and convenience. The rich rosewood paneling holds almost all the furniture required in the room. Bookshelves, cabinets, chests and display shelves take care of items to be stored or shown off; a drop-leaf bar, supported on a matching wall panel, is within easy reach when refreshments are needed. The system clears the floor of furniture, except for the black leather chair, ottoman and white occasional tables in the seating grouping, and the desk on the far wall, not shown in photograph. The chair was placed to face the TV set, also contained in a wall-hung cupboard, which slides open for viewing. The wall system permits furniture to be moved anywhere on the paneling when a change of scenery is called for. A chrome floor lamp provides adequate illumination near the chair.

HOW TO SOLVE YOUR DECORATING PROBLEMS

PROBLEM: A living room in a man's apartment with modern architectural feeling: need to create traditional look he preferred, plus lots of comfort.

SOLUTION: Unusual wall treatment for fresh architectural effect; inclusion of handsome traditional furniture.

This handsome bachelor living room started out as a bland modern room with no architectural features and a dull ambiance. Since the owner preferred a traditional mood he set about revamping the shell of the room to this end. The walls were treated to a leather-like vinyl wall covering with a mottled appearance, in soft shades of butter and brown. It was carried across three walls in a smooth expanse, but used to create a unique look on the fireplace wall. Wood panels were covered with the material and then attached to the fireplace wall, with a few inches of space left in between them. These spaces were filled in with mirrored strips for a highly original look. A large piece of smoked mirror was used over the fireplace itself for a harmonious, coordinated effect. When the walls had been treated, the bachelor owner then ran butter-colored nylon carpet over the entire floor, and this pale look underfoot stretches space by visual illusion. Furniture was chosen with care. The major piece is the handsome Chesterfield sofa upholstered in a rich tan leather. This is balanced by a table skirted in a tailored plaid cotton fabric and an antique cane-and-wood chair with a light finish. A small glass-and-brass coffee table and an antique occasional table round out this grouping. On the other side of the fireplace, the owner used two antique chairs refurbished with chocolate brown leather upholstery. Frames were stripped and refinished in a soft butter color. The fruitwood circular table between holds books and magazines. Adding a feeling of height to the relatively small room are two etageres made of brass and glass, positioned along the back wall. Utilized for books, accessories and stereo turntable, they flank a modern painting which picks up some of the colors of the room. Finished result is a charming and comfortable room with uncluttered tailored lines, ideally suited to masculine taste.

PROBLEM: *Need for total soundproofing in a small study-music room; plus modern ambiance desired by owner.*

SOLUTION: *Utilization of wall-to-wall carpet and a new wall covering with sound-absorbing qualities; selection of modern furniture.*

Comfort and the right ambiance for listening to music were the basics required by the owner of this modern den. Soundproofing was a major problem since loud hi-fi disturbed other members of the family. His solution: wall-to-wall carpeting and a new wall covering with the same sound-absorbing qualities. The carpet in bright blue is of polyester, hard-wearing and easy to keep up; the wall covering has the same soft texture of carpet and is made by the same tufting methods. The fine blue lines are simply edgings to help align the panels and would normally be trimmed off; here they were left on to add color accent and a "paneled" effect. Completing the shell are modacrylic-and-wool draperies with a translucent texture in soft white, which add a sweep of soft color at the windows. The owner built a long counter along one wall to house stereo turntable and collections of records; speakers are positioned on tall bookshelves on the opposite wall (not shown). Modern furniture introduces style and additional textures into the room. The interesting couch is made of brown leather and chrome, as are two chairs which face it across a chrome-and-glass coffee table. The small side chair is brown leather and white-painted metal. The play of art around the walls flashes the shell with just the right amount of accent color. The grouping in the corner actually continues right along this wall for a grand display of oils, prints and lithographs. A large and vividly colored painting is displayed in a novel way: it is hung on twin metal poles running from floor to ceiling; they are available from hardware stores. A modern lamp at the head of the couch and plants finish off the setting which is as practical as it is attractive.

FLOOR COVERINGS

You can put almost any material down on a floor, providing it appeals to the man in question. Most like wood floors or carpeted floors. If the room you are decorating is going to take lots of wear and tear and see heavy traffic, wood and man-made-fiber carpets are ideal, as they are durable and long lasting. Many of the synthetic carpets have the look and feel of wool and come in a wide range of colors, patterns and textures. They also clean easily and some have soil-hiding qualities. Smooth piles and short shaggy textures are the best to use, as many of the longer shags soon look messy and tangled.

Handsome area rugs create interesting effects, especially on a smooth-surfaced floor such as vinyl or wood, but it is advisable to select a rug in bright or strong colors with a fairly dominant pattern. The size of the rug should be scaled to fit the room, of course; however, stay away from fussy small rugs because they are generally not a good choice since they tend to break up areas of floor space for a cluttered look. If you use area rugs remember to anchor them in position to avoid accidents, using non-skid tape on the back of the rug. You have a wide choice of area rugs today and it's a good idea to take along the man the room is being decorated for when you shop. In this way he can see for himself the wide variety of styles and designs available and make his own choice. Foreign-import rugs include handsome selections from Morocco and Spain, usually in natural or vivid colors with a flat weave and old designs. The Danish rya rugs are generally brightly colored with long piles, and most of them come in abstract patterns. Oriental and Persian carpets appeal to some men, but these look best in traditional rooms. For this reason it is wise not to mix them into a modern scheme.

FURNITURE

The style of the furniture you select for a man's room depends of course on his personal tastes. In general men prefer antiques and antique reproductions with strong lines, especially French Provincial, Spanish and Mexican pieces, English Georgian or American traditional. Some men like the simplicity of Early American; others are more at home with the sleek look of modern furniture; some may prefer French furniture.

The actual pieces you select depend of course on the function of the room, whether it is a study, library or bedroom. Your selections should be carefully made so that you include the correct pieces for comfort and convenience. The scale of the furniture should not only be right for the dimensions of the room, but also for the size of the man. Bear this in mind when selecting such things as sofas, chairs, coffee tables and desks. Always make certain the piece is large enough, especially sofas and chairs, so that a man does not feel cramped. Remember, tall men feel ill at ease around very small furniture—avoid small occasional tables, fancy, light-scaled chairs and similar items that easily get knocked over.

A comfortable chair or sofa, recliner or rocker is a must in a man's room; select the type and style he prefers and always partner it with a good lamp on an end table or a floor lamp, for proper lighting. This is doubly important for a man who reads a great deal. If he likes to listen to music or watch television, plan for these activities when you start your decorating project. Stereo equipment and television sets are usually large in size and need to be properly positioned in a room. Make certain they are going to fit in with the rest of the furniture.

FURNITURE ARRANGEMENTS

The dimensions of the room dictate how much furniture you can include for comfort and good looks, as well as the best way to group furniture correctly. Rules for creating good furniture arrangements and focal points are given earlier in this book, in the chapter on giving a room focus. These rules obviously apply to the decoration of a man's room as well as more general living quarters. Study these rules so that you can create the most suitable furniture arrangements.

However, I think it is important to make one point clear here, regarding traffic lanes. Always be sure you have provided for traffic within the room and indicate this on your floor plan. People should be able to enter, cross and leave a room with ease, and don't forget people hate squeezing between pieces of furniture too close together. Men also like airy, open furniture arrangements, which they don't find as confining as tightly woven ones, so if space permits utilize these.

ACCESSORIES

Decorative objects help to give a room a more furnished look and a finished effect, and they are as vital in a man's room as any other in your home. If he is a collector of a particular kind of object that is decorative, such as paperweights or seals, make use of the objects in the room. Display them on tabletops, etageres, bookshelves or cabinets. His memorabilia should also be utilized, along with favorite photographs, books records and other personal treasures. They help to introduce individuality into a decorative scheme.

Good lamps are extremely important, especially in a study, den or library. Select those with strong lines in fine designs and materials; good materials to use are copper, brass, chrome, steel, porcelain, and plastic or plexiglass. Simple tailored shades look the most attractive, either in white or a solid color which harmonizes with the color scheme.

Lamps should always be strategically placed to provide the most adequate illumination, both overall and in specific areas where an activity takes place. Plan to include lamps in a reading corner or on a desk.

Wall decorations are also important, so plan to create interesting groupings of paintings, prints, lithographs, posters and photographic blow-ups, whichever he prefers and which fit your budget.

The finished result should be a room which offers a man the perfect interior environment for relaxed living—just like any other room you decorate in your home. You can create this mood and ambiance through thoughtful and skillful decorating.

PROBLEM: *A man's small bedroom requiring a revamp on a budget.*

SOLUTION: *Utilization of paint and fabric.*

This man's bedroom was once a mélange of dull beige and cream, with both colors washing over the walls, floor and bed. White window shades were dull items at the tall windows, flanked with brown shutters. The owner did a clever revamp through the use of color and pattern in paints and fabrics. He began by washing the beige walls with bright yellow paint and carried this over onto the louvered shutters. Since he could not afford to change the carpet, he left this in place, relying on the bright walls to inject the necessary liveliness into the tired room. A nature lover, he selected a fabric patterned with wild animals in tones of black and white for the bedspread, repeating this fabric on laminated window shades. This use of the print makes a strong statement in the room. To add extra color dash and contrast to the print design, the headboard and chair were covered in a richly textured tan, green and hot pink striped fabric, a handsome and unusual colorway for a masculine retreat. Brightly colored paintings and a plant add finishing touches.

PROBLEM: A basement with marred walls and floor required to function as a pool room and totally masculine retreat.

SOLUTION: Utilization of plywood paneling and carpet; inclusion of a billiard table and built-in bar.

Interior designer Jerome Manashaw was asked to create a totally masculine retreat in a dark basement, which suffered from cracked walls and a worn linoleum floor. To camouflage these he utilized light-colored plywood paneling on all the walls and put down a printed nylon carpet. The latter is firm enough to prevent distorting billiard shots yet soft enough underfoot to be comfortable for hours of standing. The easy-care carpet has a foam rubber back which adds extra cushioning. It is ideal for this all-male room because of its durability and soil-hiding properties, which make it virtually oblivious to heavy traffic. The designer found an authentic old pool table and had it refurbished. It takes the center of the room, illuminated by hanging lamps with old-fashioned green shades. For entertaining, he built an angled corner bar from wood and faced it with matching paneling; angled shelves behind it are practical and handy. The bar is serviced by tall bar chairs with cane seats. The old clock and turn-of-the-century prints are some of the accessories which add a decorative look in the handsome room, which doubles occasionally as a fun family room. Incidentally, paneling is just as easy to maintain as the carpet, requiring only an occasional dusting.

PHOTO CREDITS

Thanks are due the following for the use of photographs on the pages listed below:

PHOTO CREDITS

INDEX

259